A...

*hov...*

*through the* **HAPPIEST**

**TIMES** *of your* **LIFE**

"Reading Anita Liberty's books makes me feel like
I'm hanging out with the smartest and funniest woman
I know."                                    —*Mary-Louise Parker*

"Anita Liberty's trademark humor and cynical tone are
in top form here, but she hits a whole new emotionally
resonant stride in *How to Stay Bitter Through the
Happiest Times of Your Life,* which, surprisingly, ended
up being one of the most uplifting and authentic love
stories I'd ever read."                      —*Camryn Manheim*

"Anita Liberty's new book, *How to Stay Bitter Through
the Happiest Times of Your Life,* is fantastically funny,
seriously smart, and incredibly incisive. She's also a
really, really beautiful and helpful person. She even
wrote this blurb for me."                    —*Paul Giamatti*

*also by ANITA LIBERTY*

How to Heal the Hurt by Hating

*how to stay* **BITTER**

*through the* **HAPPIEST**

**TIMES** *of your* **LIFE**

06.06

FOR MARTHA + JOHN —

WITH GREAT FRIENDS
LIKE YOU IN MY LIFE,
HOW CAN I STILL BE
SO BITTER?
PRACTICE, PRACTICE,
PRACTICE.

THANK YOU FOR YOUR SUPPORT,
ANITA L.

how to stay **BITTER**
through the **HAPPIEST**
**TIMES** of your **LIFE**

**anita liberty**

Ⓥ   *villard*   *new york*

Author disclaimer: If I tell you that everything written in this book is a lie, how can you be sure I'm not lying about that? See? It's a problem.

A Villard Books Trade Paperback Original

Copyright © 2006 by Suzanne Weber

Published in the United States by Villard Books, an imprint of The Random House Publishing Group, a division of Random House, Inc., New York.

VILLARD and "V" CIRCLED Design are registered trademarks of Random House, Inc.

ISBN 0-8129-7619-3

Printed in the United States of America

www.villard.com

9 8 7 6 5 4 3 2 1

Book design by Jo Anne Metsch

For C.,
who really does make my life better.

Goddammit.

*how to stay* **BITTER**
*through the* **HAPPIEST**
**TIMES** *of your* **LIFE**

I am Anita Liberty. And I'm pissed off.

I am Anita Liberty—**Anita Liberty!** I am the mouthpiece for the scorned masses. I am the self-appointed spokesperson for the bitter. I am the performance poet who made a name for herself by devoting her entire career to humiliating her ex-boyfriend, Mitchell, in public when he left her for a woman named Heather. I am the author of *How to Heal the Hurt by Hating*, as it states plainly on the cover of this, my second book. I'm a cult heroine, dammit! But now I'm totally messed up.

See, my life has taken a hideous turn for the *better* and I've lost my raison d'être. I have no reason to be angry anymore. And that makes me angry. I built my entire career on being angry. It's what I do. It's who I am. But I had to go and do something I swore I'd never do—*I got over it.* What was I thinking? I'll tell you what I was thinking. I was thinking what society wanted me to think—that *happy* was the goal. Little did I know that being happy would make me so *miserable*. I'm like the little mermaid. To get the prince, I had to give up my voice. And my tail.

Anyway, here's my tale. What's left of it.

# To-Do List

Get a book published. √
Buy a nice computer. √
Rent an office. √
Launch a website. √
Pay my rent with no anxiety. √
Get a development deal with a major
    television network.
And film studio.
Get rich.
Quit temp job.
Start my own company.
Be respected for my work by certain
    conventional judges of such things. √
~~Write charming series of books about young
    boy wizard.~~ (Fuck.)

## Find boyfriend.

Make sure he turns into fiancé.
Marry him.
Write another book.
Get pregnant.
Have baby.
Get a Brazilian bikini wax.
Be in good health. √
Be less depressed. √
Be less anxious.
Figure out how to avoid death.
Become a global phenomenon.

# The Interview

Have a seat.
Congratulations.
You've passed the first test.
I don't find you sexually repellent.
You should be proud of yourself.
Most men fail that part.
Now we can begin the oral segment of the inquiry.
And if you pass that,
we can move on to the physical examination.
Ready? Okay.
Are you a registered Democrat?
Do you tell the truth?
When did your most recent relationship end? And why?
How long did it last?
What was the last movie you saw?
Do you watch TV?
Can you take a joke?
Are you generous, kind, loving?
Good in bed? Willing to go down . . .
for the paper and coffee and muffins on Sunday morning?
Are you currently in therapy?
If not, have you ever been?
And would you consider going back?
Like, say, tomorrow?
Do you understand that no one had a perfect childhood
and that the things learned during one's most
impressionable years are the tools that one uses,
the patterns one follows,
for the rest of one's life?
Do you pay your bills on time?
Do you snore?

Do you like dogs?

Do you have high standards for the things that are important to you?

Are you going to be able to deal with dating a woman who writes honestly and candidly about her life experiences and then performs what she has written to increasingly larger audiences?

Do you understand that should you and I begin a relationship, you will become part of that life experience, and that intimate, thinly disguised details of our relationship may become fodder for my act, the one performed in front of that ever-widening audience? Can you handle that?

Do you understand what I'm saying?

Do you need me to say it again?

If you do, that's all I need to know.

Thanks for coming in.

# Next.

## Excerpt from **Anita Liberty's Blog**

I am Anita Liberty. I'm sure you've got that part by now. I went through a horrible breakup and was very hurt. To get even with my ex-boyfriend, Mitchell, I decided to devote my entire career to humiliating him in public. To that end, I had thousands of postcards printed that read

and distributed them in restaurants all over New York City. I've expressed my (justified) anger in front of live and appreciative audiences in New York, San Francisco, Los Angeles, and the Hamptons. I performed my show, *Not Thinking About You,* at HBO's U.S. Comedy Arts Festival in Aspen. I wrote a book about the breakup called *How to Heal the Hurt by Hating,* and it was published by a major book publisher. National newspapers and magazines with wide circulations reviewed that book. That book is in its fifth printing. It's been published in England and Greece. Excerpts from that book are currently being used by an amazingly large number of Texas high school students for a statewide interscholastic-league poetry competition. (And one student's male speech teacher can even recite "Mitchell's New Girlfriend" by heart.) I had a short film at the Sundance Film Festival that told the story of how much I hated Mitchell. It was broadcast over and over and over and over again on cable television. And guess what? I'm still single. Isn't that surprising? Like, aren't you just shocked? Yeah. Me, too.

## Bad Dates. Good Poems.

These dates.
These men.
The ones who hurt me, bore me,
make me write poetry,
inspire me to mock them,
to examine the details of their behavior
until they are only what they are to me.
Can they all be as ridiculous as they are to me?
Or do I just refuse to forgive them for things they
haven't yet had a chance to do?

# No man stands a chance.

And I still think, foolishly, that there is a man.
A chance.
One more time for one more date to be right.
So I go
knowing that, even if it's not right,
at least I'll get a poem out of it.
A poem that snakes around the innocent boy
who sits in front of me, thinking his own thoughts,
and trying to connect and get laid and maybe even,
I'd like to think,
fall in love.
And if it's him across from me,
If he's the one,
I think I'll make fun of the one, too.

I have a lot of bad dates.
But I write a lot of good poems.

Even a cult heroine needs validation to get her through her days. So I called my best friend, Lizzy, but she wasn't in the mood to shore up her needy, self-involved, megalomaniacal friend at the moment. She was mired in the quicksand of her own self-pity. She had another bad blind date last night—and she doesn't even write poetry about it! Poor girl. So I was on my own and did what I sometimes have to do for an ego boost: ego-surf. I search the net for some sign of substantiation from a stranger. Periodically, through my website—www.anitaliberty.com— I'll get fan e-mail. Most of them are, you know, the usual: *Anita Liberty for President; You're my role model; I totally worship you; Rock on with yo' bad self;* etc. But the other day, there was one e-mail nestled in among all the e-ndorsements. It read:

> *Dear Anita,*
>
> *Get over yourself.*
> *You're just not that interesting.*
>
> *Signed,*
> *Jimster*

When your self-esteem is low and you're feeling **stuck in a rut,** your natural inclination may be to go looking for some affirmation to propel you out of your funk. It's an understandable impulse, but I'm here to tell you that sometimes affirmation is not what you need to get you to the next place. Sometimes you need the **Jimster.**

# Getting Over Myself

I'm not **always right.**
My perspective is not the **only one.**
The world does not revolve around **me.**
I could get better at hiding **my contempt.**

I'm not **invincible.**
Sometimes I fall short of **my goals.**
Some people are cooler than **I am.**
Some people are more beautiful than **I am.**
Some people are even smarter than **I am.**
I mean, I'm sure someone out there is smarter than **I am.**

**I can** do this.
**I can** get over myself.
**I'm confident** in my lack of confidence.
**I'm secure** with my insecurity.
**I'm not scared** to show you I'm scared.
**I'm strong** enough to say I'm not as strong as I seem.

No one's as strong as I seem.
No one's as great as I think **I am.**
There has to be room for improvement.
**Someone must have some advice for me.**
Next time someone gives me advice,
I'm going to think very seriously about taking it.
At the very least, I'm going to wait until they think
they've made their point before I dismiss it.

Get ready for a whole new **Anita Liberty.**

**I'll be better** than I've ever been.

Or not as good as I thought I was.

And **you'll love me** even more for loving myself less.

And, this time, **I'll appreciate it.**

I did it. I got over myself. No small feat. No easy task. No wee deed. And even though it seems to have taken a long time, the universe ultimately delivered a reward for all of my hard work.

# Good Date. Bad Poem.

He seemed nice.
He was smart.
And funny.
And cute.

I liked his clothes.

So you had one good date. With someone who seemed normal. But *seemed* is the operative word here. You never know. **You just never know.** Until you know. And even then sometimes you don't know. I dated someone for three and a half years who *seemed* normal. And then he wasn't anymore. In fact, he turned out to be extremely abnormal.

# First impressions mean nothing.

# He Called the Next Day

He called the next day.

He called. He left me a message saying that he had a really nice time and asking when he could see me again. Huh. I'm confused. It just seems so . . . so . . . *normal.* Not wanting to play games or waste time, I immediately picked up the phone and called Lizzy. She was happy for me. Happy for me in a you-had-a-good-date-why-wasn't-it-me-you-fucker kind of way. I told her it didn't mean anything. One good date means one good date.

# Another Good Date. Another Bad Poem.

He cooked me dinner.
Which was good.
And nothing he said irritated me.
Not slightly.
Not once.
And he kissed me.

That felt nice.

# He Called the Next Day (#2)

He did.
Again.

Okay. The moment of truth is upon us. A third date has been planned. It's coming up. This weekend. I'm nervous. Everyone knows what the third date means. It's time to take it to the next level. It's time to jump in and take a risk. It's time to bare all. I've been holding back. I've been waiting until exactly the right moment to open myself up.

I've told Good Date that I'm a writer. I've told him that I write about my life. What I haven't told him is that I examine the specifics of my life, most especially my dating life, with excruciating detail and perform that writing from the stage in front of an audience. What I haven't told him is that I made a name for myself by humiliating my last boyfriend.

It's too bad. It'll be hard looking at his back as he runs fast in the other direction. It's too bad, because I was kind of actually liking him.

# Good Date #3. Bad Poem #3.

We saw a movie and he held my hand.
He smiled at me a lot.
He told me I was beautiful.
He bought me a bottle of ginger ale
on the way home.
That's my favorite soda.
Guess what?
It's his, too.

I broke the news. I showed Good Date my book. I was completely honest. I made sure that he understood exactly what he was getting into.

He said that my work was amazing and hilarious and smart and that he can't wait to see me perform.

So I had sex with him.

And it was nice.

# {nice}

Mind-blowing,
toe-curling,
life-changing,
sinus-clearing,
nirvana-inducing,
anxiety-relieving,
heart-pounding,
fist-clenching,
thirst-quenching,
phone-ringing-let-the-machine-get-it-
'cause-I-could-care-less-who's-calling-
when-does-that-happen-never-or-at-least-
not-in-a-really-really-really-long-time.

## Excerpt from Anita Liberty's Blog

When we came up for air, I checked my messages and heard my manager's voice. Apparently, my first book, *How to Heal the Hurt by Hating,* was read by a creative executive at one of the largest film-production companies in the industry. In the universe. Yep. And he liked it. A lot. So he called my manager to find out about my underlying rights. My manager told him that they were still available. He was happy to hear that, because he knew an "A-List" director who might be interested in the project. Oh, and, also, he thought he knew the date I referred to on page 94. He thought he went to college with him. And here I am thinking that I've successfully disguised all distinguishing characteristics about the person who inspired that poem. Oh well. But he's not the only one who's called about my rights, to inquire if they're still available for commercial exploitation. In other words, can I still be bought? And, if so, for how much?

# {bargain}

Whatever Hollywood ends up paying
for the rights to the story of my life.

# To-Do List

Get a book published. √
Buy a nice computer. √
Rent an office. √
Launch a website. √
Pay my rent with no anxiety. √
Get a development deal with a major
  television network.
And film studio.
Get rich.

## Quit temp job.
## Start my own company.

Be respected for my work by certain
  conventional judges of such things. √
~~Write charming series of books about young
  boy wizard.~~ (Fuck.)
Find boyfriend. √
Make sure he turns into fiancé.
Marry him.
Write another book.
Get pregnant.
Have baby.
Get a Brazilian bikini wax.
Be in good health. √
Be less depressed. √
Be less anxious.
Figure out how to avoid death.
Become a global phenomenon.

It looks like everything is falling into place. Amazing. My dreams are coming true. Humiliating my ex-boyfriend in public is paying off big-time. Who knew? Actually, I did.

Now I have to do something that needs to be done. It won't be pleasant, but endings rarely are. I can't go forward into this next stage of my professional life encumbered. I made a commitment when I was feeling needy and now I'm realizing that it's time to move on. And even though it's always a difficult decision to end a relationship, sometimes it's the best thing for both parties.

# The Last Day at My Temp Job

I called this meeting
to announce
that my moment of glory is now,
my delusions of grandeur have become substance,
and **today is my last day.**

No more pretending to be interested in office politics.
No more biting my tongue at the inanity.
No more trying to make every one of you understand
that **I am better than this place.**

I escaped.
Dug a tunnel in the middle of my shift,
went toward the light,
and came out on the other side.

**I won't miss any of you.**
I don't want to remember you
or how you treated me.
As if I was one of you.
As if I should care.

Take my name off the e-mail.
Invalidate my passkey.
**Empty my drawers.**
I'd suggest bronzing my phone
as a memorial to my presence.
It's the only thing I loved about this job.
The telephone by my desk with four lines
and as many long-distance calls as I could dial.

**I will be your claim to fame.**
All of you will say you knew me when.
And I will deny it.

## Advice from **Anita Liberty**

If you're doing your own work at your temp job, maybe even writing poetry *about* your temp job, you might not want to print it out at your temp job on your last day and then get distracted by the surprise good-bye party they've decided to throw for you so that you end up leaving it in the community printer for someone to find in the middle of your surprise good-bye party. Especially if that someone happens to be Marty, the geeky computer guy who's been a temp there for over fifteen years and who has no friends. And if Marty shushes the room to read the poem aloud at your surprise good-bye party, because he's always resented your popularity and your ability to get away with doing little or no work, then that could be awkward. Really awkward. Good thing you're leaving.

## The Company I Keep

I incorporated.
I started my own company.
I am the president and CEO.
I was the first person I hired.
I decide when I need to get to work
And when it's time to stop.
I tell myself when to get a cup of coffee.
I buy lunch for myself every day.
Sometimes if things get really frustrating or boring
during work hours,

# I sexually harass myself.

I do my own Christmas shopping.
I make the holiday schedule.
I decide when to throw the office party.
And whether or not it will include alcohol.
I set the example for the dress code.
Personal calls are completely and totally acceptable,
even encouraged.
When I need a break, I take one.
I get up.
I go for a walk.

## I take a nap.

I make a phone call.
As long as I get done what needs to get done
when it needs to get done.
I choose my own salary.
I have no yearly review.
I treat myself like a human being.
I don't intimidate and regulate and berate
in order to keep myself in line.

I don't exert my authority just because I can.

## *I respect myself too much.*

In fact, I'm so happy with the job I'm doing,
I'm going to give myself a raise.

I'm a writer. A successful writer. I have achieved a level of success such that I get to spend each and every day just writing. I have a show coming up and I need some new material. (All I have so far are a bunch of bad poems about a bunch of good dates.)

So what do I do with the freedom to create? I get a big cup of coffee, turn on my computer, and play solitaire. Or I read *The Drama of the Gifted Child* for the eighteenth time. Or, let me be honest here, I think about *him*. Good Date. Mmmm. He's become the only thing I think about anymore. I stare off into space and fantasize about the day of our wedding or names for our children. I wonder if he's eating enough. Dammit. I used to have other thoughts. Interesting ones. And now that I have all this time to create and write, all I do is sit around and think about whether or not he's

*the one.*

# Advice from Anita Liberty

Get back to work.

I'm not falling in love.

I'm being dragged.

## Excerpt from Anita Liberty's Blog

I'm confused. It's been so long since I've even wanted to pursue a relationship that I've forgotten how to proceed. I feel myself starting to second-guess my feelings and scrutinize his motivations and it's all making me very, very tense. So I called someone who'd taken the plunge, committed herself fully to the man she loved, and believed she had chosen well.

# My Newlywed Sister

You got married
and now your **husband**
is your best friend
and you have all kinds
of secrets all of a sudden
that you can't tell me
and I wouldn't understand anyway
because I'm not married.

Now when I call
I have to make small talk
with your **husband**
to prove that I like him
(even though the jury's still out)
and when I finally
have you on the phone
alone, you have to go
because your **husband**
just got home
and you haven't seen him all day
(even though you spoke to each other
on the phone at least eight times
and you're going to spend the whole
evening together doing secret
married things)
and I haven't talked to you in a week
and I need to touch base
and, no, I don't think about how lucky you are
and, no, I don't think he looks like Colin Farrell
and, no, I don't wish I had a **husband** just like him.

You had a life before him, you know.
I know, because I was in it.
Don't forget,
you were my **sister**
before
you were his **wife**.

My sister's so stupid. She falls in love and is completely willing to sacrifice her sense of self. I mean, really. This is 2005. Women just don't do that anymore. Right?

## Change of Heart

Things I wanted before
I don't want anymore
because they don't involve him.

I want to pay his rent.
I want to lick his stamps
and scramble his eggs.
I want to gaze at him adoringly,
even though if anyone sees me
it will completely ruin my reputation.

I want to write the kinds of poems
he deserves to have written about him.
Poems that exalt him.
Poems that boost his confidence.
Poems that publicly glorify him.

I walk down the street
and think about how much I love him
and I feel good about all humanity.

Who the hell am I?!!!??
I don't recognize myself.
I'm not the same person I was before I met him.

# I'm totally losing my identity.

(Isn't it great?)

It's just so easy to be with him. Good Date and I have so much in common. We both like to read, watch television, eat cookies, drink milk, laugh, sleep in, feel superior, be negative, find fault, examine, criticize, get depressed, indulge our moods, introspect, take issue, resent, hold a grudge, and take long walks on the beach.

It's like we were made for each other.

Went out with Lizzy and Samantha last night. It had been a while. I think they resented that. Well, at least Lizzy resented it. She's the one who feels left behind. Lizzy's accusing me of dropping off the face of the earth. She's not wrong. But I know she'd be the same way if she met someone who didn't repulse her. But she hasn't. She's still single and misses both whining about and exalting our single status together. I've become one of "them"—the happy ones—and that naturally puts distance between us. I told her that she should know me better than that and that this is sure to come to some fiery, horrible conclusion sooner or later, but she's not comforted by the thought. She's convinced I'm going to marry Good Date. I don't know why she'd jump to that conclusion. Sure, I'm almost in my mid-30s and haven't felt this way about anyone since Mitchell, but we all know how well that turned out. Besides, Good Date's just a good date. A really good date, but a good date all the same.

On the other hand, all Sam wants to hear about is the sex. She says that she and her husband have basically become Best Friends with Benefits. And the benefits aren't coming as fast and furious and frequently anymore. I just realized something. Could Sam be the Ghost of My Relationship Future? And could Lizzy be the Ghost of My Relationship Past? Interesting. Scary, but interesting. I loved hanging out with my friends. I did. But I missed Good Date. I swore that I'd never be one of those women who as soon as she hooked up with someone found it difficult to tear herself away from him for even one evening so she could hang out with the friends who were indispensable to her through many, many lonely nights. Oh well. I'm allowed to enjoy the fact that I'm so close to being happy. I know it won't last and maybe that's why I'm savoring it. These rose-colored glasses will shatter. Problems will arise. Flaws will surface. Reality will set in. I would be nervous, but I've never been one to shy away from reality.

## Fool Me Twice

I'm an idiot.
How could I have let this happen?
I should have been more aware.
I let my guard down.
This time, I'm the fool.
It was going on
right in front of my face,
under my own nose,
frequently in my own bed.

And she knew exactly what she was doing.
She knew he was taken.
She knew he was mine.
But she moved forward anyway.
Flirted.
Lusted for him openly.
Never hid her desire.
## *That bitch!*

She has no shame.
She lies seductively on her back,
immodestly splaying her legs in the hope that he'll notice her,
that he'll touch her in that place that makes her feel
like such a good girl.
I know that trick.
I taught her that trick.
Rewarded her with a biscuit when she performed it
on command.
Now she's using that trick against me.

She looks at me while she's licking his sweat-soaked skin.
Sticks her tongue out at me while he's stroking her belly.
Growls when I try to move her out of the way
so that, maybe, just maybe,
I could have sex with **MY BOYFRIEND.**

And it's not like he's completely innocent.
He leaves her messages on my machine.
Tousles *her* hair after he and I have made love.
Whispers sweet nothings into her ear.
Makes her come.
## Stay.
## Beg.

He told her he loved her.
Although he hasn't yet said it to me.

I didn't do anything to deserve this.
I've always treated my dog well.
Cared for her, fed her, protected her.
And I've never, not once, tried to steal *her* bone.

**bad dog**

I performed tonight for the first time in front of Good Date. I have to say, it was a great performance. No, it was a transcendent performance. I was on. I was *it*. Afterward, people gathered around me, praising, adulating, fawning. I appreciated the accolades, but I wanted to find Good Date. I wanted his praise, his adulation, his fawn. I spotted him at the bar. He gave me a huge, warm smile. I approached him and silently practiced a humble response to his reverence: "No, really, you really liked it? You thought it was amazing? Come on, the best thing you've ever seen on the stage? That can't be true. Okay, okay. Don't get upset. I believe you." When I got to him, he took me in his arms and kissed me deeply. "So," I murmured, "what'd ya think?" He tells me he thought it was great. "And?" I smile.

"And I have a few notes."

# "NOTES?"

"Yeah," he says. "We can talk when we get home."

We're gonna talk when we get home, all right. Because clearly he doesn't understand that the last person who tried to give me notes . . . was the first person who tried to give me notes.

# {defensive}

Why does this word have negative connotations?
Being defensive is actually a good thing.
It's certainly a good thing in sports. And in driving.
And in physical combat.
Sometimes one has to do what one has to,
to protect oneself.
Against the other team, another driver,
an opposing force, an intruder . . .
or unsolicited criticism.
Being defensive is different from being overly sensitive.
(I'll admit to being defensive, but I am not overly sensitive.
**I'm not.**
Stop looking at me. Go away. Turn the page already. Jeez.)

## Excerpt from Anita Liberty's Blog

Well, that's a milestone. Our first fight. It had to happen
some time. I think it went pretty well. I enjoyed it. I didn't
talk to him the whole way home. That irritated him. When
we got home, I told him that I was pissed about how he
responded to my show. He told me I was being too
defensive. I said that being defensive was appropriate
when someone performs for the first time in front of the guy
she just started seeing and his first reaction is to criticize
her performance. He said that he wasn't criticizing, he
just had a few "suggestions." I told him it was too early
in our relationship for him to be giving me advice about
my work, when I'd been doing my work *just fine* without
him for years. He said that maybe I just couldn't handle
constructive criticism and that that was a good thing to
know about me. I said that maybe he was just threatened
by my talent and my success and that that was a good
thing to know about him. He said that he was just trying to
help. I said I'd let him know when his help was needed.
He said that that hurt his feelings. I said that he hurt my
feelings first by being anything other than completely
positive and enthusiastic about my show. He apologized
and said he didn't want to fight anymore. I pouted. He
apologized again. He said that my show was amazing
and it was incredibly sexy to see me onstage doing my
thing and knowing that he was the one who got to go
home and have sex with me. I told him that he shouldn't
have counted his chickens. I then asked him what
"suggestions" he had. He didn't want to say, but I pressed
him. And, ya know, they weren't bad. The guy actually
had some good ideas. He then went on to tell me, in
detail, how beautifully the show flowed together and how

well it was structured and how funny and smart I was, etc. He also said that he was relieved that we were still in the phase of our relationship where I was writing nice poems about him and not critical ones. He said he didn't know how he would handle that. I just smiled.

# He Needs Help

I wonder if there's a support group
for the loved ones of self-confessional performance poets.
How do they cope?
Could they give my new boyfriend some tips?
>If I were a photographer, I'd take his picture.
>If I were an artist, I'd paint his portrait.
>If I were a sculptor, I'd mold his bust.

But I'm a negatively inclined performance poet
so I write poems about
>his encyclopedic knowledge of **porn stars**
>the way he sits on the couch and proclaims fearlessness
>of **extreme sports** without ever actually having
>participated in any of them
>his pathological **inability to find his keys** when
>they're seriously right in front of him
>the fact that he considers *The Life and Times
>of Eugene Debs* a beach read

and then perform them live in front of an audience
of family, friends, and strangers.

I try to explain to him that it could be worse.
He could inspire **nothing at all.**

I hate to be a whiner, but relationships are *hard*. I forgot how *hard* they are. How being with another person brings up all these *issues* and you start to settle into patterns of behavior that you then realize aren't healthy, so you have to break them, but that feels weird, because now you're used to the role you're playing and anything different seems superficial, even if it's healthier. And you have to think about things like how to present your needs such that you don't sound needy. Here's what I know about relationships: **They end.** Falling in love means you can fall out. I have a boyfriend and I know what that means. In the blink of an eye, the stroke of a pen, the push of a button, that boyfriend can just as easily become an **ex-** boyfriend.

# {reassurance}

He said he wouldn't leave
unless we're fighting every day,
at each other's throats, and
unable to function responsibly apart or as a couple.
And I realized something.
If he wasn't going to leave until that point,
he would be standing there alone.
Because I would be long gone.

## Excerpt from **Anita Liberty's Blog**

I'm the poster girl for the Society to Mistrust the Longevity of a Romantic Relationship (better known as **SMLRR**). And, yet, here I am. Trusting again. Loving again.

They're going to revoke my membership. And getting reinstated is a bitch.

Boyfriend and I are going away for the weekend. We're going to Vermont. To a cabin. In the woods. Away from everything. And everybody. Just the two of us. No distractions or interruptions. It was his idea. Me? I live for distractions and interruptions. Lizzy asked me if I thought Boyfriend had planned this romantic weekend because he's going to propose. I was like, **"What?** Propose? Are you crazy? We've only been together for a few months. I'm not going to get engaged after only a few months of knowing someone." Lizzy said that she knew that I wouldn't, but she didn't know about him. So it got me thinking. I mean, he does talk a lot about our future together. He talks about things very far into the future. He acts like it's a given. It does seem like he's ready to take the next step, even if it seems quick. I've heard stories of people who "just knew." I never thought I'd be one of those people, but maybe I'm about to go on a romantic weekend with one of those people.

## Advice from Anita Liberty

Be aware that sometimes well-meaning friends can unwittingly (or wittingly) plant a tiny thought in your brain that, finding your brain to be a fertile and hospitable environment, can germinate and sprout and take root and spread and grow and flourish until you have no more room in your brain for any other thoughts. Especially rational ones.

We're back. The first night we were there, we sat on the couch and drank red wine. We were staring deeply into each other's eyes. There was a fire blazing, crickets chirping, the promise of a hot night of sex in front of us. Everything was perfect. All of a sudden, Boyfriend gets this *look*, like something has occurred to him. Like this moment is a special moment and he has something he wants to ask me. I swear. That was the look he gave me. So he looks at me meaningfully and tells me to wait on the couch, that he has to "get something." He gets up and walks across the room to a trunk in the corner. My heart dropped into my stomach. My throat constricted. I'm thinking, "Oh my God, he's getting a ring. How'd he get a ring into that trunk in the corner? He hasn't been out of my sight since we got here. I even peed with the bathroom door open. Oh! I know. He FedExed a ring to this place and had the owner hide it in this trunk so that he could retrieve it and propose. Now that I think about it, I'm quite certain that the owner gave Boyfriend a little conspiratorial wink when we checked in." I was a little drunk at this point, so I'm trying desperately to separate out my immediate panicked reaction from my actual feelings and I'm finding it extremely difficult. I'm like, "Okay, I now have about thirty seconds to figure out what I'm going to say when he asks me to marry him. Do I want to marry him? Can I tell him it's too soon and that we should get to know each other better? Will that hurt his feelings? Should I just say yes and see how that feels? Maybe it's not too soon. Maybe we are meant to be together. If he knows, maybe I should trust that. Maybe I should trust him. That would be a novel concept."

Boyfriend closes the trunk. I'm shaking at this point, anticipating what's to come. He turns to me, smiling. And he's holding . . . a *blanket*. That's right. A *blanket*. He sits down beside me and puts it cozily around us. He says, "That's better. I knew there'd be one around here somewhere. Hey, you look really pale all of a sudden. Are you all right?"

I gurgle, "Uh, yeah. Fine." I am relieved. Oh, and strangely disappointed. (Or is it: "I am disappointed. Oh, and strangely relieved"?)

## Advice from **Anita Liberty**

I don't care what people say.
I don't care that sometimes it works.
You just cannot possibly know whether
you want to marry someone you've
been going out with for less than a year.
And I might even say two years.
You can't know for sure.
And why would you want to?
What's the rush?
Where's the fire?
This isn't a race, dammit.
So much happens in the first year
of a couple's relationship that can
inform the rest of your interaction,
why add the pressure
of committing yourselves to
each other for the rest of your lives?
Because it's romantic?
Because you want social acceptance?
Because it's something exciting
in the midst of your all-too-routine life?
Because it's something?
Not good enough.
It's Relationship Roulette.
Sure, it might lead to a happy ending.
But it might also blow your relationship's brains out.

Got a call from my manager. The "A-List" director wants to meet me, so his film studio's flying me out to Los Angeles. Also, there's a **network executive** who's interested in developing my work into a **television show.** I'm going to L.A. next week to take lots and lots of **meetings** with lots and lots of **important people.**

I'm excited to get my brain back on track. I've been spending too much time thinking about **Boyfriend** and **our relationship.** I mean, why am I even worrying about one person's commitment to me when I'm really interested in a much **larger following?**

# Ode to a Mainstream Audience

Oh, you amorphous, fantastic, elusive object of my desire.
Most mysterious assemblage of conventional acceptance.
You tease me, Mainstream Audience, tempt me with
your approval,
with the wideness of your congregation, the variousness of
your community.
To have audience with such an audience,
to be heard, nay—dare I wish't—to be understood by you.

Oh, Mainstream Audience, nation of hatchlings, yearn for
my words!
Cry out for more of me!
Demand that I fill your belly and wash your brain.
This is the hunger that drives me further from my home.
I seek this audience, because of its magnetic magnitude,
its grand gamut.
Imagine't. Each congregant given the gift of seeing
the world through my eyes.
Nary any one deniéd the occasion to see that I am always right.
'Tis what the planet needs, what it e'en deserves.

Liberty is the elixir poiséd to addict this common
and uncomplicated audience.
And, oh, Noble Duke of Burbank, you will be
my implement of deliv'ry.
Soon to depart the days of sermons to the converted in
theaters downtown.
The declaration of Liberty will be exhorted on national television
and in first-run cineplexes.

I dare not sleep until Mainstream Audience has had me—
And I have had my way with it!
Onward! Unto the West, to brave whate'er impediments are
placéd in my path!

# To-Do List

Get a book published. √
Buy a nice computer. √
Rent an office. √
Launch a website. √
Pay my rent with no anxiety. √

## Get a development deal with a major television network. And film studio.

Get rich.
Quit temp job. √
Start my own company. √
Be respected for my work by certain
  conventional judges of such things. √
~~Write charming series of books about young
  boy wizard.~~ (Fuck.)
Find boyfriend. √
Make sure he turns into fiancé.
Marry him.
Write another book.
Get pregnant.
Have baby.
Get a Brazilian bikini wax.
Be in good health. √
Be less depressed. √
Be less anxious.
Figure out how to avoid death.
Become a global phenomenon.

## Excerpt from **Anita Liberty's Blog**

I'm in the **Chateau Marmont!** I was flown first class to L.A.! There was *a car and driver* waiting for me at the airport! There were warm nuts on the plane! Warm nuts! Up until now, I've only had cold nuts. At best, room temperature. I've arrived and I will never go back. And now I'm one of those people who stays at the Chateau Marmont. I walk around like this is natural for me. Like I always stay here. Like I need to stay here. And I do. I need to stay here. Sure, I miss Boyfriend. It would be really nice if he were here to . . . oh, Derek, **my masseur** is here. Gotta go.

## Excerpt from **Anita Liberty's Blog**

I have a meeting tomorrow with the "A-List" director. (I have to stop and ask, who makes up this "A-List" anyway? I bet there are a lot of people who think they're on the "A-List" who aren't. Or who are, but shouldn't be.) Mr. A-List wants to hear my ideas. Huh. Time to come up with some. Because all I know so far is that the screenplay I would like to write is one woman poet's treatise on the socio-politico-emotiono-spirituo-physical dynamics of heterosexual interpersonal non-platonic relationships at the commencement of the 3rd millennium.

And a heartwarming romantic comedy.

EXT. CHATEAU MARMONT—DAY

ANITA LIBERTY, an adorable redhead in her ~~mid~~
early thirties, sits poolside at one of the
most celebrated hotels in Hollywood. She wears
sunglasses (of course), and a bikini (of
course), and she sips a large iced chai latte
(of course), which has been brought to her by a
HANDSOME WANNABE ACTOR who can't help but gaze
at her loveliness and feel dismay at her
obvious lack of interest. Anita's cell phone
rings. She flips it open.

> ANITA
> (into phone)
> This is Anita.

INT. STRETCH LIMO—CONTINUOUS

A dark-haired man wearing sunglasses sits in
the back of a limousine. He speaks through a
very tiny headset. He's in his mid-thirties.
You can smell his cologne. This is MAX DALTON.

> MAX
> (into headset)
> Anita? Anita Liberty? This is Max Dalton.

EXT. CHATEAU MARMONT—CONTINUOUS

Anita takes a sip of her large iced chai latte.
A flicker of recognition crosses her face.
(Intercut phone call.)

> ANITA
> Yes. This is Anita.

                          MAX
I heard you were in town.


                          ANITA
You heard? From whom?


                          MAX
Ya know. It's around. Your book has people
talking.


                          ANITA
              (practicing humility)
Really?


                          MAX
Oh, yeah. And, well, see, I'm a producer. . . .


                          ANITA
             (sitting back in her chair)
Look, Max, it's very nice of you to call,
but I'm already committed to another
producer. I mean, we got so many calls
and, ultimately, I went with . . .


                          MAX
Actually, I'm friends with Jack.


                          ANITA
Jack?


                          MAX
You guys went out.


                          ANITA
We did?

                    MAX
For a while. Like, a couple of months.

                    ANITA
Not ringing a bell.

                    MAX
He's a professor.
                    (beat)
He has dark hair.
                    (beat)
He wears glasses.

                    ANITA
Oh! Jack! Huh. Interesting. Well, either
way, I'm still committed to this other
producer. . . .

                    MAX
Jack's getting married.

                    ANITA
Great. I appreciate that you're . . .

                    MAX
I'm putting together his bachelor party.

                    ANITA
Okay . . .

                    MAX
And I was wondering if you might, well, if
you might want to be involved.

Anita, who has taken another sip of her large
iced chai latte, almost chokes.

                              ANITA
          Involved? Involved how?


                              MAX
          Ya know, I just thought it would be really
          funny if you could maybe, I don't know, if
          you could show up and perform something.


                              ANITA
          I'm sorry, you want me to "do" a bachelor
          party?


                              MAX
          Yeah, like maybe you could do some
          material about Jack.


                              ANITA
          Material? I don't have any material about
          Jack.


                              MAX
          But you must.


                              ANITA
          Oh, I know. What about if I also jump out
          of a giant cake wearing pasties and a
          G-string?


                              MAX
          We'll pay you.


          Anita hangs up her cell phone in disgust. Even her
          large iced chai latte tastes bad. She stares off
          into space and thinks about what might have
          happened had she said, "Sure, that sounds like **fun.**"

INT. HOTEL ROOM——NIGHT

A bunch of clearly inebriated guys sit around a
luxurious hotel room. The remains of an indulgent
room-service dinner is in evidence. There are a
number of empty bottles of champagne, bourbon, and
other types of liquor scattered around. There is a
knock at the front door. Max jumps up to get it.
JACK, mid-thirties, dark hair, glasses, and the
man of honor, falls back on the couch drunkenly.

>                    JACK
>              (feebly protesting)
>     Oh no. What's this now? A stripper? Please
>     tell me you didn't get a stripper.
>     Kathleen will kill me.

>                    MAX
>     It's a surprise.

Max opens the door and a waiter wheels in a
cart covered in a white cloth. He pushes it to
the middle of the room. Max gives him a tip and
the waiter leaves.

>                 MAX (cont'd)
>     Okay, everyone, have a seat. I have
>     something special prepared for Jack.

The guys all sit down on couches and chairs.
Max picks up a corner of the white cloth.

>                 MAX (cont'd)
>     Gentlemen, hold on to your hats. You're in
>     for a very special performance. This woman

is in demand and very, very good at what
she does. She's a professional.

The guys start getting excited. Especially
Jack.

                    MAX (cont'd)
          I have the pleasure of introducing . . .
          Anita Liberty!

Max pulls the cloth off the cart and Anita jumps
up wearing her usual uniform, a nondescript
T-shirt and jeans. There is silence as the guys
realize that she is not what they were expecting.
Especially Jack.

                    JACK
          Anita?

                    ANITA
          Hey, Jack. How are you?

                    JACK
                  (awkwardly)
          Okay. Little drunk. How're you?

                    ANITA
          Doing pretty well. Hey, congratulations on
          getting married.

                    JACK
          Uh, thanks.

                    ANITA
          I've prepared a poem for the occasion.

                         JACK
          Oh my God. You didn't. Wow!


Jack settles in for the show. Max sits looking
pleased with himself. Anita pulls a piece of
paper out of her pocket and begins to read.


                        ANITA
          I call this poem "Memories of Jack."
              I remember Jack.
              Well, most of the time.
              If someone reminds me.
              Once, while I was dating Jack,
              a friend asked me how Jack was,
              and it took me a good five minutes
              before I knew who the hell
              she was talking about.
              Exasperated, she finally said,
              "Isn't that the name
              of the guy you're dating?"
              "Oh! Jack."
              Jack's a sensitive man.
              Very sensitive.
              He cries.
              A lot.
              At almost anything.


Jack is looking less and less comfortable. His
friends are laughing. He is not.


                    ANITA (cont'd)
              Once, he cried because I wouldn't
              walk with him in the rain.
              I had a new leather jacket and
              a friend with an umbrella, but

```
                    Jack took this personally.
                    Very personally.
                    Jack wouldn't let my dog up
                    on his bed.
                    Jack needed constant reassurance.
                    Jack told me he knows
                    how handsome he is.
                    Jack has a lot of hair on his butt.
                    But the thing I think
                    is most important
                    to know about Jack is that
                    he sleeps in a nightgown.
                    Not a nightshirt.
                    I can tell the difference.
                    He sleeps in a nightgown.
                    I'm not kidding.
```

Jack's friends have been laughing throughout, but
at this final bit of information, the room is
silenced. Jack looks terribly uncomfortable. Max
looks regretful. Anita looks satisfied.

```
                    ANITA (cont'd)
              Thank you. And good night.
```

INT. CHATEAU MARMONT—CONTINUOUS

Anita smiles, settles back in her lounge chair,
and turns her face up to the sun.

## Excerpt from **Anita Liberty's Blog**

There's something about L.A. that can make a relatively young woman feel relatively old. So I'm dressing like I'm 25. Low-cut jeans, sparkly barrettes, sheer peasant shirts, the whole deal. And my manager invites me to this party where everyone is dressed like a 25-year-old (because they *are* 25) and even though I've dressed the part I feel so old and I can't figure out the party dynamics or where I fit in and I don't know how to be sexy and cute anymore and I can't even flirt, because now I have a *boyfriend.* So there I am, not wanting to dance, not able to flirt, but still craving someone's attention so that I can go home (alone) feeling good about myself.

Finally, I just give up and decide to go home (alone) *not* feeling good about myself. I'm on my way out when I see Jodie Foster walking in. Jodie Foster? What's she doing at this party of 25-year-olds? She's older than I am. But then I see that she's just passing through the party to get to the private dining room in the back of the restaurant. I try not to stare, but she is a celebrity and I can't help myself as I walk by. I look at her. And . . . she looks back. Her eyes lock with mine. And I swear it's a *meaningful* look. A look full of meaning. She smiles the gentlest hint of a smile. It's like we instantly have a secret. And I don't think it's just the secret that we're 10–15 years older than everyone else in the room. I think we have a *connection.* And that she thinks I'm cute. And gay. Or at least bicurious. And I am . . . curious. But before I have a chance to consider my options, she's gone. Jodie Foster wanted me (I'm quite certain) and now she's gone.

Okay. My night is saved. I call Boyfriend from outside the party. He picks up on the first ring and I can immediately tell that we're in different cities, different time zones, and very different mind-sets. I mean, I went to a party where I practically had hot sex with Jodie Foster and he stayed home and watched reality TV reruns. He sounded depressed. It really brought me down. And I was way the hell up there. It was a bummer. And that's the thing about relationships. You're not always in the same place. I'm amped in L.A. and he's unplugged in N.Y. And I'm not pulling out my plug for anyone. I have work to do. I have goals to reach. I have markets to saturate. I have dreams to realize. (Especially the one where Jodie and I are stuck in an elevator, just the two of us . . . ) And I have a big fabulous meeting tomorrow to talk about my movie.

## People Who Want to Make a Movie of the Story of My Life and the Things They Say That Make Me Say, "Wait . . . What?"

The story of your life needs to be more **commercial.**
Performance poetry is not **commercial.**
No audience is going to want to watch someone talking onstage in front of a mike for an hour and a half.
In the movie,
Anita Liberty can't be a performance poet.
She can be like, maybe like, *she can be a fashion designer.*

We're hungry for **a late-twenty-something revenge comedy,** but we don't want Anita to exact her revenge by humiliating her ex-boyfriend in public.
That's too mean.
And, in general, **we think Anita's too angry.**
She needs to be shown doing something nice for someone.
And Mitchell's perspective has to be sympathetic.
And Mitchell's new girlfriend, Heather, oh,
what if Heather is a brain surgeon?
Or what if, maybe, what if Anita just thinks Heather's a blond bombshell, but, in fact, it's revealed in the end that **Heather's a black woman?**

In the end, Mitchell and Anita should get back together.
In the end, Anita and Heather become best friends.
In the end, Anita Liberty should realize the error of her ways.
In the end, Anita Liberty will be played by **Hilary Duff.**

# {control}

Once you've been labeled a "control freak," then anytime
you express an opinion about how to do something
a certain way, you're dismissed as being that way
that you always are, even when you're right.
*Even control freaks are right sometimes.*

Some things I know how to do.
## Really well.
And I know that I know how to do them.
## Really well.
Does that make me a control freak?


(By the way, that was a rhetorical question.)

Wow. What a huge mistake. Mr. A-List turned out to be **Mr. A-Hole.** At this "creative" meeting, at which I disagreed vehemently (but politely) with several "ideas" that were suggested by Mr. A-Hole's 20-something, blond, large-breasted assistant, Mr. A-Hole asked his girlfriend (who's kidding whom?) to leave the room and he yelled at me. **He yelled at me.** He told me I was being difficult and that there were no bad ideas (though, actually, I could rattle off several hundred that have come up since I walked through the door of his office this morning) and that I wasn't going to make it in this business unless I was willing to compromise my original vision in order to serve the larger picture. I just sat there—numb and bemused. I didn't respond. He then got flustered and realized that he might have come down a little hard on me, so he tried to lighten the mood. He tried to flatter me and soothe me—the way a torturer dresses the wounds he himself has inflicted on the tortured, such that the tortured comes to appreciate the torturer as both her punisher and her savior. Mr. A-List laughed off his tirade and then made me promise that I would never write **a poem about him.**

## A Poem About Him

If you didn't want people to know that you're a dick,
you shouldn't have been a dick in the first place.
Especially not to a woman who has devoted her entire career
to publicly humiliating the last dick she encountered.
What were you thinking?
You can't fly me first class to Los Angeles
under the auspices of helping me to execute my vision,
laud the freshness of my voice,
celebrate my raw talent,
and then yell at me for not doing it the way
it's always been done.
You told me I was disposable.
That writers like me were a dime a dozen.
That you were doing *me* a favor.
You said this all
with your sunglasses on.
You took three calls.
You ordered breakfast.
Scrambled egg whites.
(Hey, if the facts were mine to make up, I'd have you
be less of a cliché than you are.)
You said you could walk away right now
and leave me with nothing.
You don't scare me.
I've been here before.
I know what it's like to be rejected,
knocked down, dragged out.
I know how to get up, dust myself off,
and turn it all to my advantage.

I will go on living my life
with or without you in it.
And I will never bend to your authority.
You see, I don't care about protocol.
Or the hierarchy of your tiny fiefdom.
You can't expect me to defer to authority for what you have
to offer.
Which, it turns out, is nothing.
People have been trying to teach me that for years and look
where ignoring
it has gotten me.
Look up. Further. A little further.
Can you see me yet?
Helloooooo!!!! I'm heeeeeree. Up here. Above you.
Way, way, way over

# {career}

I'm at the end of my rope.
No, I'm past the end of my rope.
I can no longer even see the end of my rope.
I don't even remember what the end of my rope looks like.
Did I ever even have a rope?
What's a rope?
R-rrr-r-ooo-oo-p—e?

## Excerpt from **Anita Liberty's Blog**

I was thinking of calling my next book *Anita Liberty Does Hollywood and Hollywood Doesn't Even Say Thank You*. However, I'm now realizing that that's not really the most accurate title, since it doesn't seem that I'm done doing Hollywood. My next book should really be titled *Anita Liberty Is Doing Hollywood When She Notices That Hollywood Is Staring at a Point in the Middle Distance and When Anita Liberty Asks Hollywood What It's Thinking About, It Says, "What? Oh, Nothing."*

# Excerpt from Anita Liberty's Blog

Called Boyfriend. The phone sucks. There are all these long pauses and silences and you don't know what the hell the other person is doing on the other end, but he sounds distracted and distant and you're not connecting even though you really needed to hear his voice and get some support and then maybe you hear the telltale beep from his computer and you know that he's either playing solitaire or surfing the net. I hung up on him. (What? I'm in L.A. I'm feeling dramatic.)

He called back and was apologetic and I got to feel superior and self-righteous for a few minutes. And that felt good. Being apart is hard. Especially at this point in our relationship. We had a really nice momentum going and sometimes space is good and sometimes space bites you on the ass.

Ow.

Hollywood is giving me some kind of mind-fucking and I'm practically begging them not to stop. It's just that in the beginning it feels so good. It makes you feel so special, so loved, so recognized, so deserving of that recognition. And then Hollywood turns around and tells you you're unlikable. People like me. I have a boyfriend. So at least one person likes me. Most of the time.

Since things in the film arena weren't working out the way I wanted, I moved on to television. I had never written a sitcom pilot before, so the network wanted me to work with someone who had. Apparently, writing a sitcom pilot is a lot like flying a plane. You can't go up there by yourself unless you've put in the hours with someone who knows what he or she's doing. Otherwise, someone could get hurt or die. Also, writing a sitcom pilot is incredibly difficult and complicated and even though you may have written a book and numerous one-person stage shows and a short film and content for a website and magazine articles and a screenplay (almost), you'll never figure out how to write a sitcom unless you learn the secret handshake of mediocrity. But I can't go into this with a bad attitude. This is a fresh start and a network sitcom could afford me an enormous arena in which to reach the masses.

The network paired me up with a team of experienced writers. Two women. I was relieved because I thought that women would better understand my voice and my point of view and be more nurturing and encouraging of my process. Mr. A-Hole left a small fissure in my self-esteem and I needed some female energy to help repair it. Also, these were two women who had made it in a field that's dominated by men. I felt I could learn from them.

I was thrilled to be working with them. Honored that they wanted to work with me. Excited by the thought that they would help me to execute my vision and deliver my ideas to a mainstream audience. And one of them is pregnant. For the first time, it comforts me, the sight of a fecund female across from me. I can relate, because I, too, am pregnant.

# {pregnant}

Pregnant with ideas.
Pregnant with possibility.
Pregnant with creative potential.
Pregnant with the fruit of my labor!

When Boyfriend and I first got together he told me about this female friend of his named **Emily.** I paid her no mind. Why would I? I was in the luscious throes of the nascence of a new relationship. I was not going to be shaken off my perch by **Emily.** Even an adorable brunette with a great body who used to spend entire weekends with Boyfriend after they graduated from college, sleeping in the same bed, getting drunk and stoned and satisfying each other's need for companionship (but, oddly, not sex) between romantic relationships. No, that wasn't going to bother me back then. I was too confident *back then*. There is no greater confidence than that founded on the back of baby love. (And feel free to quote me on that.) You're untouchable, invincible, safe. It actually warmed me when Boyfriend told me about **Emily** and how just two weeks before we got together, he had drunkenly told **Emily** that he thought he might actually be in love with her after all and that he thought they were supposed to be together. As he drank, he poured out the contents of his heart. He told her that he'd always been attracted to her and that maybe the reason neither of them had found anyone to settle down with was that they were meant to be together. I smiled and laughed at that story, because I was the one lying naked, postcoital and precoital (it was the same thing *back then*) in his arms. He told me about **Emily** in the context of expressing his gratitude at having found me. He was telling me how close he came to making a huge mistake. And included in the story was the greatest reassurance of all: **Emily** turned him down. Flat-out rejected him.

Why do I bring up **Emily** now? Why does **Emily** rear

her perfectly tousled head at this juncture? What does **Emily** have to do with anything? Well, since you asked . . . Guess who's been spending a lot of time with Boyfriend since I left for L.A.? Guess who was there tonight when I called? Guess who I heard playing with *my* dog in the background as Boyfriend tried valiantly (but unsuccessfully) to keep up his end of our phone conversation? Guess who I heard burst out laughing just as Boyfriend was hanging up the phone?

# Emily, Emily, Emily.

When Boyfriend told **Emily** he wanted to be with her, she told him that he was sweet and would make a great boyfriend, but that she didn't want to compromise their friendship. Yeah, right. Clearly, she just wasn't that attracted to him. But now that he's got a girlfriend, maybe she's decided that she is that attracted to him. Maybe the thrill of the chase is what does it for old **Emily.** Maybe she needs competition to hold her interest. Maybe the object of interest needs to seem more desirable through someone else's desire. Now that I desire him, maybe she'll start desiring him, too.

I have to focus. Where would I rather be? In Hollywood finally getting the recognition I deserve? Or in New York figuratively mud-wrestling some flaky chick named **Emily** for the prize of Boyfriend? I've met with industry bigwigs. I've had lunch with studio heads. Jodie Foster wants to take a long cool drink of me and I'm worried about **Emily**? Eyes on the prize, Anita. Eyes on the prize. And the prize is global recognition, not **Emily**'s best male friend.

# A Letter from Anita Liberty

*Dear Emily,*

*How ya doing? It's me, Anita Liberty, your best male friend's current lover. Or the woman who's now got what you didn't want until it belonged to someone else and now you're reconsidering. I just wanted to go over a few things, since I am sort of taking over where you left off.*

*First, let me say up front that I am not one of those women who are on a hair trigger about their boyfriend's female friends or ex-girlfriends. (I'm not sure in which category the ambiguous nature of your relationship with my boyfriend lands you.) I'm not easily threatened. I'm not overly possessive. I did have a terrible experience in my last relationship, where a woman came along and pulled the boyfriend right out from under me. But one bad apple doesn't have to spoil the bunch. I like women. Some of them are my best friends.*

*Second, since it looks like I'm here to stay, for at least the next long while, I was wondering when you could come and collect the influences you left on my boyfriend's life? Because they are going to have to be removed no matter what. By force, if necessary. Don't get me wrong. I'm not unappreciative of the time you put in, the reassurances you gave, the TiVo box you bought, but it's my turn now, Emily. Just back away from my boyfriend slowly and keep your hands where I can see them.*

*It's not like I don't know how you feel. I do. I can relate. I have male friends. I have ex-boyfriends. But*

*now that I've moved on, I think you should, too.*
*Believe me, you don't want it to get ugly. Just quietly*
*take back your feelings of superiority and your*
*I-knew-him-first-so-I-know-him-best attitude and*
*let me get on with his life.*

> *Sincerely,*
> *A.*

What the hell was I thinking? These two women are worse than any white male in white linen eating egg whites. At least Mr. A-List is man enough to wear his cliché on the sleeve of his Armani suit.

But these two?!?! Women, yes—in that they have vaginas (I'm assuming) and breasts and a Y chromosome (maybe they share one between them)—but not human females. They're sharks. In soft, pastel-colored, warm, and fuzzy costumes. I was fooled into thinking that they might be easier to work with, that they might be the ones who could nurture and accept and encourage and hearten. I mean, one of them is pregnant. Pregnant! She's going to have to nurture someone. Or something. At some point. Soon. She's going to have to figure it out. Or maybe she's the type of animal that eats its young.

We had breakfast together at a very fancy restaurant in Santa Monica. The two of them sat there across from me, over their steaming bowls of steel-cut oatmeal with Craisins and organic raw sugar, and told me what the "character" of Anita Liberty would and wouldn't do. It was a lot of fun, really. Then they informed me that they would be writing the first draft by themselves, that that's the way they work best. Even though there was all kinds of talk of collaboration when we first met, it's now two against one (or three against one, if you count the fetus). And I'm back in high school again. The law of numbers. They're the bullies and today I'm the target of their contempt. But I'm not in high school. I'm a grown woman and I can be reasonable. I can reserve judgment. (Not really, but let's pretend.) Maybe their first draft will be great. Maybe it will surprise me. Part of collaboration is knowing when to let go. (Or so I've heard.)

All in all, for my first interaction with them post–contract negotiation, I think it pretty much sucked.

## People Who Want to Make a Network Sitcom of the Story of My Life and the Things They Say That Make Me Say, "Are You High on Crack Cocaine?"

We want to see the world according to Anita Liberty.
We want to see Anita dealing with the world in a unique
and different way.
We love Anita's point of view, but we don't want to show the
genesis of that point of view;
i.e., we don't want to see her go through a breakup.
And we're not going to want that point of view to be
as pointed as it is anyway.

We can't have too many plotlines
that revolve around Anita Liberty.
The characters can't read too real, too grounded in reality.
We need to just go for what's funny.
Wackiness is funny.

We can't have a scene where Anita confesses her true feelings
about her sister's wedding to her sister's caterer.
Because it's too big a scene to have with a guest star.
And since he'll never appear in a future episode, there'll be
no reason to care about him.

The network made a deal with you because they think
you have a fresh voice.
They say they want something *different*.
**Sitcoms have gotten too formulaic.**
However, if you try to write something that veers too far from
the formula, we're going to put you in a creative choke hold

and won't let go until you turn in something we recognize,
so that we can then tell you that it reads too much like a
traditional sitcom.

And that's not why the network hired you.

Come to think of it, we're not sure why they hired you.

But now that you're here, can you go get us a
Frappuccino?

## Excerpt from **Anita Liberty's Blog**

So I got the first draft of the Anita Liberty sitcom pilot written by two women, neither of whom are Anita Liberty, and guess what? Are you ready for this? It's truly shocking, so you might want to sit down or hold on to something. . . . It totally fucking sucked! We did some work on it. They let me participate in rewriting, but only minimally, and there was only so much I could do without tying them up, grabbing the laptop, and running. We just handed it in to the network. And now we have to wait for the news about whether the sitcom about Anita Liberty (or these two writers' completely bastardized version of Anita Liberty) is going to go.

*Spoiler alert:* It's not going to go.

But I am.

# Leaving on a Jet Plane

I'm leaving L.A. tomorrow.
I'm going home.
I'm heading back east.
And my pride is going with me.

Well, it's not exactly going with me.
It's going UPS Ground and it's still costing a fortune.
I couldn't afford overnight delivery.
Not two-day. Or even Priority Mail.
My pride is a heavy load.
It's also fragile and takes special handling.
What it has cost me to send my pride back home,
you have no idea.
It will take two to three weeks to arrive.
Maybe four.
Maybe seven.

But at least I will get it back.
Hopefully in one piece
and only slightly worse for the wear.

## Excerpt from **Anita Liberty's Blog**

On the plane back to New York from Los Angeles. Wouldn't you know it? My nuts are cold. At least I still have nuts. But they're definitely not as toasty as they were on the way out.

As soon as I got home, I called my new television agent to find out what happened with the Anita Liberty pilot. And she says, "The Anita Liberty pilot? That's dead. So maybe you'd like to think about pitching something else." Something else? Pitch something else? **I don't have anything else.** That's the point. This was it. And if this isn't going to take me to the top, then I'm just going to spend the rest of my life bottom-feeding. Something else? **I have nothing else, you fucking moron.** I am Anita Liberty. I write what I know. And this is all I know. And everyone thought it was pretty fucking fantastic for a while, so I wasn't thinking that I'd have to have other ideas. **I have no other ideas.** I'm not kidding. **Nothing.**

And, once again, I turned to the Internet for comfort. I needed to ego-surf. Just to reassure myself that I am someone. Someone important. Someone who means something to strangers. Someone other than the person who's a dime a dozen, dead in television, and who has no other ideas. Someone whose name shows up 2,820 times on the Web. Thank God for the Web. Because I found exactly what I was looking for. It was the online diary of a teenaged girl whose screen name is *danipuke*. *Day-nee-puke?* Or maybe she pronounces it *donny-poo-kay*. She has several lists: favorite movie stars, favorite TV shows, favorite CDs. I clicked on the list of her favorite authors. It read as follows:

Kerouac
Burroughs
Ginsberg
Vonnegut
Anita Liberty

If you're thinking of going to L.A., you might want to

# stop.

# To-Do List

Get a book published. √
Buy a nice computer. √
Rent an office. √
Launch a website. √
Pay my rent with no anxiety. √
Get a development deal with a major
   television network. √
And film studio. √
Get rich.
Quit temp job. √
Start my own company. √
Be respected for my work by certain
   conventional judges of such things. √
~~Write charming series of books about young~~
   ~~boy wizard.~~ (Fuck.)
Find boyfriend. √
## Make sure he turns into fiancé.
Marry him.
Write another book.
Get pregnant.
Have baby.
Get a Brazilian bikini wax.
Be in good health. √
Be less depressed. √
Be less anxious.
Figure out how to avoid death.
Become a global phenomenon.

# {sabotage}

Since I seem to have lost control of my career
for the moment, what else can I conquer
and build and rule and feel capable of
single-handedly destroying?

What's that? My relationship? Hmm . . .

There are things I don't like about him. I have to admit that. He's not perfect. But are his flaws flaws that I can live with for the rest of my life?

We haven't stopped fighting since I got back from Los Angeles. He's just so moody. And that would be fine, but I'm moody, too, and our moods aren't in sync. At all. His mood ring is black when mine is rosy. His is blue when mine is all swirly green. His goes white when mine goes purple. It's one thing to deal with the unpredictability of my own mood swings, but to have to deal with another person's? It's getting to be too much. Am I just scrutinizing him in preparation for taking the next step? Or is it simply that he's

# **not** *the one?*

When is it time to let go?
To be happy with what you have?
To stop wanting what you don't?

In my case, it would take a
# prescription.

## Excerpt from **Anita Liberty's Blog**

Boyfriend and I have shared everything, every thought and feeling, up until now. And now it seems like there's some sort of unspoken contest going on between us to find out if we're both heading toward the same goal at the same time without articulating exactly where we each are in our journey. I mean to say, in the beginning of the relationship it's all "Oooh, I feel this way and that way and do you feel this way and that way, too? And isn't it great that we feel exactly the same way at the same time and we get to share in each other's process?" And the milestones—the first time you have sex, the first I-love-you's, the first discussion about long-term goals and the future of your life together—the steps forward and the steps back, all still leading you, inching you closer to making the ultimate commitment to a life spent together. It's all shared. Of course there continue to be clues and hints and rhetorical questions, but *the* question—*that* question—has to be asked and answered internally first. For oneself. Alone. "Do I want to marry this man?" Regardless of what kind of risk that entails? Regardless of what *he* wants? Obviously it's a possibility or I wouldn't even indulge myself by asking the question. That question wouldn't even be a question unless we were in some kind of position for me to ask it and not feel foolish. So I ask myself again, "Do I want to marry this man?" I think so. And that's all I can come up with. It should be a resounding *yes*, shouldn't it? Sometimes it is a yes. And sometimes it's a maybe. Because there is no knowing for sure. I do know *that*, that there is no knowing for sure. It's all a big "Gee, I *think* I can make this work." And those who go into this union any other way are fooling themselves.

And the rest of us.

# Advice from Anita Liberty

Damn the people who have no doubt.

So Boyfriend and I got into a huge fight. My birthday's coming up and I panicked about my age and the state of our relationship. Embarrassing, but true. It didn't help that I've been feeling fairly underappreciated in terms of my career these days. Hollywood can't seem to make a commitment to me, so someone better. Basically, I freaked out and, in my freakitude, I tried to dig out some kind of reassurance that things were going to be okay. "Okay" for me in that moment meant . . . it meant that someday, sooner rather than later, we were going to get engaged. So, without directly asking him to marry me or asking him to propose, I expressed my concern about the forward progression of our relationship. It wasn't pretty. That I know. Whatever I said, in whatever squirrelly way I managed to say it, exacted this response from him: "You're not sitting around *waiting* for me to propose to you, are you?"

No. No. (Yes. Okay, yes.) No, not really. It's not like that. (Yes, yes, I am. And why should I be ashamed about that?) No! Why would you think that? I'm a feminist. **I am a feminist.** I have to be a feminist. I rail against tradition. I intellectualize the mechanisms of the intimate dealings between two people who love each other. I'm working toward intimacy and communication on a higher plane. A person like that, with those as her goals, that person doesn't sit around waiting for her boyfriend to propose. And yet . . .

And yet I find myself sitting around waiting for my boyfriend to propose. We've articulated all that we can, short of "We're getting married." And we stop short of that because, well, because he's supposed to say it first. He's supposed to know it first. And then I can see how I really feel about it. It's like a big complicated game of chicken. One of us must go first. One of us must put ourselves on the line. Why him? Well, let's see . . . I am the one who has to carry any children we might decide to have by myself for nine months and then suffer the pain of childbirth.

All he's got to do is ask a stupid question and get a
# stupid answer.

# Advice from **Anita Liberty**

You're in a relationship.
It's been going pretty well.
But you're starting to have
some doubts, some questions.
Until you're clear on what
answers you want to hear to
those questions, keep those
questions to yourself.

## Excerpt from **Anita Liberty's Blog**

Boyfriend thinks I'm acting out. Boyfriend thinks I'm projecting my own fear of commitment onto him. Boyfriend thinks I'm just freaking out because I'm about to be 35. Boyfriend thinks that the more invested I get in the relationship, the more I pull away, because I'm scared of being hurt again. Boyfriend thinks that I'm trying to turn him into the villain so that if things don't work out, I can blame him and I don't have to take any responsibility for my own behavior. Boyfriend thinks I'm so busy preparing myself for the worst-case scenario that I can't see that what we have is solid and real and wonderful. Boyfriend thinks I've camped out in the negative place so that if things go wrong, I can always soften the blow for myself by being able to say that I saw it coming. Boyfriend thinks I'd rather be right than happy. **Boyfriend's right.**

But I'm not telling him that.

# {irony}

My boyfriend has become Mr. Relationship.
And I'm like: Don't get better than me at this.
This is what I do. I define myself by my ability
to name and analyze what goes on between
two people involved in a romantic coupling.
You can't be better than me at this. ***It's not right.***

It's my birthday. My 35th birthday. I'm 35.

# 35.

I thought I would feel smarter and more grounded at this age. I guess I imagined that feeling and watching myself age wouldn't matter because I'd have achieved inner peace and be filled with self-love and experiential wisdom. Or, at the very least, I'd be married. Or famous. Or rich. Or someone's mother. Nope. It's still just me. Getting older. Alone. Struggling. And still hating my life most of the time. I only want what everyone else has. Because it looks better. And faster. And shinier.

Everyone makes such a big deal about turning 30. 30's no problem. ***30's cake.*** 30 feels like an accomplishment. At 30, you still have time. Now, 35 is a different story altogether. 35 is the new 30 (until I turn 40 and then that will be the new 30). I believe 35 is now the age where one takes stock, evaluates, looks back, panics, and despairs. Especially if one is a woman with a boyfriend whom she loves and who she knows loves her back and he's younger than she is and seems utterly, utterly unconcerned with her increasing age and the effect that may or may not be having on her reproductive system.

At my birthday dinner, Boyfriend asked me a

# big question.

## My Name's Anita and I Have a Problem

I thought I was very clear about my time frame.
What I needed to happen when I needed it to happen.
I thought I told you that I had a problem,
born justifiably from experience,
with cohabiting without a promise.

# I'm sorry.

I really would like to be able to abandon that
archaic and traditional example of a future together, but, um,
I had a bad experience before. A breakup.
One that occurred very shortly after I moved in with the guy.
I don't know if I've mentioned him before.
I don't know if I've told you the story.
I tend to be kind of withholding of the details of my
past relationships.
His name is **Mitchell.**
We went out for three and a half years
and then we moved in together
and, four and a half months later, he left me for another
woman?
Named **Heather?**
Oh, you *have* heard the story.
Oh, you *saw* the short film.
You *logged on* to the website.
You *read* the book.
You're *familiar* with the one-woman show.

# *Okay* then.

What still confuses you about how that one experience affected
virtually every moment in my life from that point forward?
Reasonably including the way I deal with romantic relationships

and my ability to trust their durability in the face of the work
needed to make living together a healthy and pleasant and
satisfying move to make.

# I'm not scared
of taking the next step toward commitment.

# I'm scared
of taking the next step without witnesses.

Boyfriend's never lived with anyone before. He's never set up a home with someone he loves. He's never experienced a relationship on a 24-7 basis. But I have. Oh, have I. And I liked it. The living-together part. It was the being-dumped part that I wasn't so very fond of. A couple has to experience living together before they can know whether or not to take the next step. You can learn a lot about someone by living with him, by building a home with him. I've always believed it was a necessary step in a relationship, part of the natural progression for a couple in today's world. Oh God. But if things don't work out this time, I think I'm gonna . . . No.

# They're going to work out this time.

# {optimism}

Ummm . . . it's . . . uh . . . let me think . . . I . . .
Oh, never mind. I can't even fake it.
I have no idea what this word means.

## Excerpt from **Anita Liberty's Blog**

We moved in together. No proposal. No promises. Nothing. He told me not to worry, that he wasn't going anywhere. Whew. That's a relief. (Maybe I should type my sarcastic comments in a different font so you'll know how to read them.) I just feel like I'm having relationship déjà vu.

**I've been here before.**
I've given up my apartment.
I've trusted my instincts.
I've put extraneous items in storage.
I've combined my CD collection with someone else's.
I've gotten rid of duplicate books.
I've bought fresh new sheets.
I've ordered pizza and eaten it on boxes the first night after the move.
**I've trusted someone.**

Boyfriend's right. There's no reason to worry. Why would I worry? IT'S NOT LIKE THE LAST TIME I MOVED IN WITH SOMEONE HE TURNED OUT TO BE A SOCIOPATH OR ANYTHING. (By the way, my sarcasm font is Copperplate Gothic Light.)

# Excerpt from **Anita Liberty's Blog**

I'm going crazy. Every week that goes by, every romantic dinner, every time Boyfriend reaches for me lovingly, I think, "This is it. It's about to happen. He's going to ask me to marry him." I can't help myself. I can't stop the train I'm on. I loathe the woman I've become. I want to mock the woman I am. I'm fixated. And, more than the desire to get married to Boyfriend, I'm mostly just driven by **the need to know**. It's the *not knowing* that's eating a hole in my brain. I really don't like the idea that he may know something about the future progression of our relationship before I do. Well, I actually don't like him (or anyone) knowing anything about anything before I do.

One thing about moving in together is that he has a subscription to *The Nation* and I have a subscription to *Entertainment Weekly*. I like that magazine. A lot. I just do, okay? And I like to read it from the beginning to the end. First. But now that I live with *someone*, my *EW* comes in the mail and *someone* takes it and starts flipping through willy-nilly and, if that weren't bad enough, *someone* starts pointing out bits of information and quoting from articles so that my precious virgin read is completely ruined.

Boyfriend simply does not understand my frustration with this aspect of his behavior. He thinks I'm just being neurotic, as if idly dismissing my neuroses will make them go away. *Ha!* I'm like, "It's my subscription! You subscribe to *The Nation*. Whose fault is that? I can't help it if my magazine is a Cinnabon compared to your stale dry toast of a read. It's *my* Cinnabon! You can't sit there on the couch and eat it, *from the middle,* and tell me how good it tastes. I don't want your dry toast. I don't want actual, political, useful information. I want celebrity gossip and insider Hollywood analysis. I wanna know what the best new fall TV shows are. I wanna know what the celebs are wearing to Sundance. I wanna know who's expecting a baby and what Madonna brought to the shower. And I wanna know before anyone else in the apartment.

# Is that so wrong?"

## Life, Liberty, and the Pursuit

# Sitting on a futon couch,
in this tiny one-bedroom apartment,
with a small white fluffy dog at my side,
**listening** to Sarah McLachlan,
## drinking coffee,
## eating chocolate pound cake,
and ### *recording* my thoughts
on a PowerBook G4
# *trying* to convert my vertiginous point of view
into some sort of sharp-edged
commentary on the mundane occurrences
that string together into an undirected
and unplanned way of life.
# Nothing interesting here.
What's wrong with me?
I used to think that every thought that
bubbled up in my brain warranted
examination and expression.
# Not anymore.
Now I can't think a thing
without rolling my eyes
back into my head
as if to give my cerebrum
a dirty look.

I'm no longer interested in the process. In fact, it bores me. I feel like I know all I'm ever going to know. But haven't I thought that at every juncture, every step, of my life? That this was the end point. I felt it at 30. Felt it at 28. Felt it at 21. Let's be honest: I felt it at 14. That I was capable of running my own life. Why the dip in confidence? Why now? Now when everything (okay, at least more things than before) is moving forward? The goal appears to be caring less about the incidentals that make up the waking hours of every day. But the stakes are getting higher. The desire for stability only **grows** and becomes more elusive at the same time. It seems that way anyway. I realize that I've found most of what I thought I was looking for. And now there's no more drama. No more temp jobs. No more dates to make fun of. I could care less about my ex-boyfriend, Mitchell. So I'm a little bored. And sleepy. I'm gonna go take a nap.

# Excerpt from **Anita Liberty's Blog**

Boyfriend keeps asking me what's wrong.
I keep saying, "Nothing."

# {nothing}

Something.

I'm totally getting cold feet. That's what this is. I really don't want to be single again, but it's almost the abhorrent thought of it that makes me want to run screaming into the center of that fear. Like a moth to a flame. It's hypnotic. On the other hand, maybe my feet are cold because I'm finally seeing a long-held goal come within reach. And I don't know what I'll do without the dogged pursuit of romantic satisfaction and happiness. What will drive me? I'm scared of getting what I want. I'm scared of not getting what I want. I'm scared of not *knowing* what I want. Or realizing that what I thought I wanted is not what I actually want. What?

My boyfriend asked me to change my look.

To something other than **contemptuous.**

## The Calming Down of Anita Liberty

# I've started taking yoga.
I am the cobra, the cat, the corpse.
I pull up on my mula bandha.
I center my chakras.

# I meditate.
I acknowledge the negative thoughts
and then push them away.

# *I burn a type of incense*
called "Quiet Mind."

# **I drink Tension Tamer tea.**

# I went on the pill.
To make me less moody.

# Nothing seems to work.
Because, in yoga,
I look through my third eye
and this is what I see
(besides an hour and a half
of not being able to check my voice mail):
I see that my negative thoughts are going to make me a
household name.
I see that it's the noise in my mind that fuels my art.
I see that if my tension is tamed, my career will be over.
And that if my moods don't swing, my agent will drop me.

I see that the only way
*I'm going to achieve inner peace*
is to do whatever I have to
to avoid it.

## Excerpt from Anita Liberty's Blog

For me, the worst thing imaginable would be to believe in the durability of my relationship to such a degree as to feel it was invincible and then get blindsided. That would hurt. A lot. So I'd rather just prepare myself by doing the emotional equivalent of waving a big stick around in the middle of a pitch-black room after hearing a suspicious sound. And, hopefully, I'll hit whatever the thing is that may be about to put a knife in my back. Am I really that scared? Scared to the point of paranoia? Or am I psychic? Do I feel something inevitable coming? Or do I feel nothing at all?

I don't trust him anymore. I've turned the corner. The corner that I seem to turn in every relationship. Nothing is good enough. Nothing is enough. I mean that. That's not an exaggeration. What could someone do to convince me that he really loved me? And would be faithful. And would always be there. And wasn't judging me. Marry me? I'm not that much of an idealist. Or am I?

## Excerpt from **Anita Liberty's Blog**

I finally confronted him. It was like an emotional earthquake. The pressure just built up until something had to give. I said that I was sick of pussyfooting around the subject of us getting married. I felt like I was walking on eggshells and that I was tired of apologizing for my feelings. I'm a 35-year-old woman in a serious relationship. It's perfectly normal and natural for me to feel ready to take the next step. I don't want to be made to feel like I'm just a passenger in my own relationship anymore. I need to know if he's ready to make a lifetime commitment to me and our future together. And I need to know it now. I told him that if he still wasn't ready, that I was going to call it a day. And that he should be man enough to be honest with me and let me move on with my life.

He said that, in fact, he couldn't tell me at this very moment that he was ready to get married. And if I needed to go look for someone who was more ready than he was, that he'd understand. (N.B.: He seemed pretty fucking ready when we met, back when it was just an element of our foreplay, to talk about the day of our wedding and spending the rest of our lives together, but now that the time is now . . . but whatever.) He said he didn't want to hold me back. And if I had to **go,** I should **go.**

**So.**

I should **go.**

# anita's state of mind right now

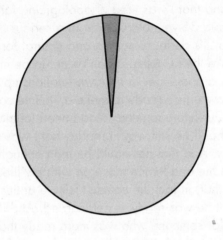

Right
Happy

## Excerpt from **Anita Liberty's Blog**

We've decided to take a break. Somewhere between my breakdown and our breakup. It was a mutual decision. And it's supposed to be temporary, but maybe only to forestall the inevitable. I said I didn't want to go on if this wasn't the real deal. He said he didn't want to feel pressured into making one of the biggest decisions of his life. This hurts, but it's better than getting dumped on my ass without warning. Again. It's always better to just rip the Band-Aid off quickly and suffer the pain in one big jolt, as opposed to trying to slowly pull out each one of my hairs one by one. I've been waxed. I'm familiar with the pain involved.

Lizzy and I went out last night. I was a barrel of laughs. Lizzy was actually great, welcoming me back warmly into the fold. Maybe a little too warmly. I won't say she's happy about this turn of events, but I think the idea of me settling down into a nice, healthy relationship was rocking her world. It was certainly rocking mine. Maybe I'm not giving her enough credit. At the very least, I will say that she seemed energized by the crisis. But, then again, I could be projecting. As painful as this is, it's given me something to focus on, to analyze and dissect.

# I Told You So

What is it about those four words that makes
them roll so deliciously off the tongue?

*I told you so.*
*I told you so.*

Left over from the playground,
taunting other kids,
recognizing the position of power
that being able to see into the future affords you.

I knew it!
I was right!
I'm psychic.
I saw it coming, even if no one else did.
*Especially* if no one else did.

The respect,
the glory,
the accolades.
She's so smart.
Nothing gets by her.
No one can put one over on her.
She never gets surprised.
Or blindsided.
By anything.
Or anyone.
Ever.

I may not like what I see,
but I see it coming a long time before anyone else does.
I see it first
and that's the prize.

Note to Self:

Fulfill prophecy.√

Not knowing what else to do, I bought a candle. It was a Fortune Candle. You're supposed to burn it until a small charm is revealed. It comes with a little guidebook that tells you what the charm signifies. I lit the candle and sat on the couch and waited. And waited. And waited.

It's a big-ass candle.

I could be here forever.

This is ridiculous.

I simply don't have the time.

I need to know my fortune now.

So I got my cuticle trimmer from the bathroom and started gouging out huge chunks of warm wax until I found the charm. It was an elephant. Consulting the guide, I'm told that the elephant charm represents romantic stability. In getting it out prematurely, I broke off its trunk.

It's easier to go back to *fantasizing* about perfection . . .

than to accept that perfection is just a *fantasy*.

## Excerpt from Anita Liberty's Blog

I went out with Samantha last night. Lizzy was supposed to join us, but the cute guy whom she's been flirting with at work finally asked her out on a date. And so the torch is passed. And now I'm the one who's free on a Saturday night. Aaaah, the cycle of life.

Anyway, it was good to hang out with Sam. She's married. She's happy. She likes her husband. She got a good one. I was sitting mournfully in front of my mojito and railing about the state of my life. I told her I'd never find anyone who was willing to go the distance with me, how I kept making the wrong choices even when I felt like I had my eyes wide open, how I felt destined to repeat the same relationship pattern again and again and again. I said that I knew that I shouldn't have moved in with Boyfriend. It was all a big mistake. I told him it wouldn't work out. I told everyone it wouldn't work out. Sam asked me what it was I actually wanted. I said I wanted security. I wanted stability. I wanted a vow that someone would love me forever and ever and never go away. Sam said she understood my wanting those things, especially after what I'd been through with Mitchell, but that none of those things are guarantees. All of a sudden, I realized that I sounded like a child. I know all this. Intellectually, I know that everything's a crapshoot. Emotionally, I'm still 13 years old and believing that marriage is forever. I have friends who've gotten divorced. I was at their weddings. Weddings where eternal love and devotion were vowed. I know that at a certain point it's all a giant leap off a cliff into the unknown.

I think I just leapt off the wrong cliff.

# Advice from **Anita Liberty**

If you're in a great relationship
with someone who respects you
and you're ready to get married,
but the person you're with isn't,
break up with him.
That way you'll eliminate
any possibility of getting hurt.
Or being happy.

# Advice from **Anita Liberty**

Whatever you do,
don't take my advice.

## Excerpt from **Anita Liberty's Blog**

He hasn't called me. Not once. No e-mail. No text messages. Nothing. He's gone radio silent. And that can't be good.

## Excerpt from Anita Liberty's Blog

I have to give him his space. I'm not going to call him. He'll call me when he's ready. Right? I just have to be patient and wait.

*(Five minutes later . . . )*

Still haven't called him.

*(Four minutes later . . . )*

Picked up the phone. Put it down again.

*(Seven minutes later . . . )*

Okay. I called him. What? I waited. For sixteen whole minutes. I'm not a machine. I have to say, he seemed a bit distant and distracted, but he agreed that we should get together to talk. I don't like the sound of that. He's coming over tonight. I said we could meet on neutral territory, but he said it was easier to just come over here. He probably wants to pick up some things.

## Excerpt from **Anita Liberty's Blog**

Boyfriend came over and I started to talk, scrambling to find the words to fix everything. He interrupted me and said that he wanted to go first, that he'd been thinking a lot about things (oh shit), and that he had some things he wanted to say. He stood up and took out a piece of paper and read me the following poem:

### I'm Not Mitchell
by Anita Liberty's Boyfriend

I'm **not** ugly.
I'm **not** a liar.
I'm **not** a coward.
I'm **not** fooling myself.
I'm **not** going to make promises
I don't intend to keep.
I'm **not** a sociopath.
I'm **not** emotionally stunted.
I'm **not** pretending to be something I'm not.
I'm **not** going to lure you into a false sense of
security and then pull the rug out from under you.
I'm **not** Mitchell.
And I'm **not** going to dump you for another woman.
Or for any reason.
Ever.
As long as I live.

I was speechless. He looked at me expectantly, proudly, anticipating my response. Finally, he asked me what I thought. I told him I thought it was great.

He wanted more. "And?"

"And I've got a few notes."

He laughed.

I told him that I, too, had been doing a lot of thinking and that I had come to the realization that I had been putting too much emphasis on getting engaged. I didn't want him to feel pressured in any way. I said that I wanted to be with him no matter what and that I was willing to allow things to be organic and spontaneous and to just see where the road takes us. (It was like speaking French. And I don't speak French.)

He nodded and said he appreciated and understood everything I was saying. He just had one question. . . .

# Finally!

I'm engaged!
I have a fiance.
I'm going to have a husband.
But first, I'm going to have a wedding!!!
I'm getting married.
I'm getting married!
I'm going to be a bride.
I'm going to get to wear a **white dress.**
And walk down an aisle.
Have a shower.
Wear a ring.
Choose attendants.
**Arrange flowers.**
Make favors
**I'm engaged!**

(Cut along the dotted line and remove this page entirely
from the book. The poem printed on the other side of this
page honestly conveys my initial reaction to getting
engaged, so I felt that it was relevant and responsible to
include it, but it's really embarrassing. The book is fine
without it. Cut it out and dispose of it. Shred it. Burn it.
Flush it down the toilet. Just get rid of it.
You'll be doing all of us a favor.)

I told my parents tonight that I'm getting married. They were thrilled. A little too thrilled, actually. They, who have never put pressure on me, have apparently been harboring some parental desperation. I always thought that they were being so cool, so mellow, not expressing any anxiety about my lack of husband or baby. But now I realize that they've been gritting their teeth and hoping beyond hope that I'll fucking find someone already and settle down and pop out a grandchild or two. My mother asked if I was planning on having a wedding. A real one. She's learned not to take anything for granted with me anymore. When I told her yes, she smiled and nodded and said that that sounded nice. But I knew that what she really wanted to say was

# "Finally!"

## Excerpt from **Anita Liberty's Blog**

I have a secret. And it's not pretty. But it's the truth. And it must be told. Since Boyfriend and I got engaged, people are nicer to me. My family certainly seems to like me better. And I'm enjoying it. But it's not like I'm not conflicted about it.

Not only do I feel like I'm betraying my still-single friends and the single people in my audience to whom I derided the conventions of coupledom, but I also feel like I'm betraying myself. I made being single an empowering choice I was actively making. I enjoyed the life I had crafted for myself. I made a career out of it. Now I feel like I've completely sold out. And here's the hard part to admit . . . I like it so much. I want everything that comes to me with this decision that ~~Boyfriend~~ Fiancé and I have made: the wedding, the gifts, the social acceptance. I never even wanted an engagement ring before. Before when I thought I was never going to have one. And now I want one. Bad.

# Ring It On!

The engagement ring.
I love the ring.
White gold.
Small diamonds.
A circle of loveliness.
A band to beat the band.
It looks like a wedding band.

And I like that.
Maybe that's all I needed.
To look married.
At the gym.
With those big mirrors.
Lifting weights with my hands,
with my fingers, one of which
sports a wedding-band-type ring.
I know others notice it.
Because I notice others.

And I know they think,
"Oh, look at her, she's working out and taking care of herself
and she's so cute *and* married. She's got a husband. Someone
who loves her. The proof is right there on the third finger of her
left hand."
I know they think that, because I used to think that
about others.
Before I was one of the others.

And I would look at women with bands and think,
"She found someone and I can't? What's up with that?"
So I'm assuming there's at least one person who's looking at
my left hand and thinking, "She found someone and I can't?"
And I, with all the empathy and compassion I can muster,
want to shout across the room . . .

# "Damn right sister!"

## Excerpt from **Anita Liberty's Blog**

I told Lizzy that Boyfriend had changed his name to Fiancé. It was hard. She seemed happy for me. She acted happy for me. I tried to tone it down, but how do you tone down the news that you're engaged? I didn't want to have to temper my enthusiasm, but I know how she feels. God, do I know how she feels. How many times did I pick up the phone after excruciatingly lonely weekends and hear my coupled friends announcing their inevitable engagements and/or pregnancies? How many times did I watch my spring and summer calendar fill up with the inconveniently weekend-long festivities celebrating other people's good fortune? How many times did I get creamy, calligraphed invitations addressed to me and a "guest" and know that I had no such "guest" to accompany me? How many times did I get an invitation addressed to me and me alone? I get it. Oh, do I get it. I know Lizzy feels like the last one on the team to get chosen. And I know that I feel like a last-minute draft.

I would say that the only downside to getting engaged, for me, is the thought of being inextricably linked to another person. I mean, that's really hard when you're a solo performer. When you've always done your best work alone. When you're a performance poet who speaks uncensored to paying audiences about the minutiae of her life. My life. The thing is, now that I'm *betrothed,* I have to start thinking more in terms of *our* and less in terms of *my.* And that's hard for me. Since I've started processing the details of my life in public, I haven't had anyone in my life I needed to protect, anyone whom I *wanted* to protect. And I'm understandably concerned about how that will affect my work. I am nothing if not my process. My ability to process and comprehend from a point of view that is specifically and uniquely mine is what makes me, well, me. And then the ability to convey that version of the events that make up my life to an audience. It's always worked. I don't want to change the formula. It is my purpose in life to translate my experience into exhibition, to name names, to be indiscreet, to call the kettle black. It's not just my job, it's my *calling.*

## What if getting married fucks all that up?

It's **not about** being a l o n e
to write . . . **it's about** writing
about *not being* a l o n e .

# {math}

Atlantic City.
I have $100.
Fiancé has $100.
I'm up $80.
Fiancé is down $120.
Now that we're engaged,
are we both down $40?
That would suck.

Being engaged has changed me in many ways. For instance, I've had to retire my **i hate him** hat since I've found myself in a relationship with someone I respect. If I wear my hat when I'm out with Fiancé, it's sort of the same as wearing a T-shirt that says: **i'm with stupid.** And I'm not. Anymore.

# Return of Sex-Guy

It's not what you think.
I would <u>never</u> . . .
I mean, at least not again.

The phone rings.
The machine picks up.
A voice not heard for years announces its return:
"Remember me?"
Do I ever.
## He's Sex-Guy.
And you can never forget Sex-Guy.
No matter how hard you try.

He's heard there's a poem about him.
He's heard that he's inspired art.
He's not scared.
He's FLATTERED.
## He's Sex-Guy.
And he's got a motto:
"No press is bad press."

Of course he hasn't read the poem in question.
So I call him back and deny that he's the inspiration.
If he's not going to be offended,
I'm not going to enjoy the admission.
And if I'm not going to enjoy the admission,
why admit?

But ## he's Sex-Guy.
And he's nothing.
If not persistent.

He tells me to send it to him anyway.
I tell him to go buy the book.
He tells me he just wants to read this one poem.
He gives me his e-mail address.
I promise to send it to him.
I am energized by making a promise I know I won't keep.

## But he's Sex-Guy.
And he's not put off by broken promises.
Vows not kept.
Favors not done.
What does he care?

## He's Sex-Guy.
And his ego provides him with all the reassurance
he'll ever need.
He never receives an e-mail from me.
Because I never send one.
So he calls me again. And again. And again.
I don't return the calls.
I just don't.
And that . . . is pretty fun.
Leaving his numerous calls unanswered is, in itself,
a bonus for a poem well written.
I finally feel rewarded for enduring
the experience of him in the first place.

## It's a tie, Sex-Guy.
You: One. Me: One.
A draw.
And I did it without really even trying.

## He's Sex-Guy.
He was bad in bed.
Oh. And look:
He's just as bad out.

I can't *let go of old* **resentments** Nor do I really **want** to.

It seems that when you're engaged and you meet someone else who's engaged, you immediately . . . engage. It doesn't matter that in any other circumstance, you wouldn't spend five minutes talking to this person. All of a sudden, you're discussing marriage, religion, family dynamics, monogamy. With a stranger.

I met a woman who's getting married this June and we immediately jumped into a discussion about planning our weddings and all the feelings that it was bringing up. I talked about how weird it was to finally be doing something I thought I was only going to fantasize about doing for the rest of my life, about those lonely years camped out on my futon trying to prepare myself for a life alone. How, after having, on some level, succeeded at convincing myself of the bravery of making the choice to be alone, planning a wedding now feels like a certain betrayal of that self from five years ago, and so I'm constantly struggling with these two seemingly incompatible and inconsistent sides of myself. This woman nodded knowingly and agreed sincerely, and I felt comforted by her ability to relate. Then I find out she's 25.

25.

Just how could she possibly begin to understand what I'm talking about when I spent a full decade more than she did with my ass glued to my futon?

# A DECADE.

# Advice from Anita Liberty

Don't engage.

## Excerpt from **Anita Liberty's Blog**

My hair is thinning. I found a tiny bald spot on my hairline a few weeks ago and I started examining it every few days or hours or so and now I actually feel like all of my hair is thinning. Like I can see way too much of my scalp. Especially when I get out of the shower. I've never had thick hair, but I was never concerned about seeing my scalp before. And, all of a sudden, it's all I can think about.

I asked Fiancé if he noticed my thinning hair, but he said the only thing he could possibly say, which was, "What? Of course not. You look beautiful." No help there.

I never realized how much one's hair has to do with one's sense of self. My self-esteem is going down the drain—literally!—so I brought it up to my therapist. I told her that I was scared that I was going to go bald. My therapist told me I wasn't going to go bald and suggested that I might just be transferring some of my anxiety about being engaged to a fear of loss of innocence, aging, and death. Whatever. Anyway, she said that I didn't look any different to her and asked me to tell her what I saw when I looked in the mirror. I thought about it for a minute and then said, "I see some sort of scruffy, gnomelike creature with just a shot of wispy hair." She nodded sagely and wrote something down on her yellow pad.

## Excerpt from **Anita Liberty's Blog**

I went to a dermatologist today so she could tell me that my hair-thinning fears were all in my head. When I arrived, I was told to take a seat in her office so we could talk before she examined me. So I sit down across from her enormous desk. I mean, this desk is fucking huge! And she asks why I'm there. And I say, "Well, ya know, I don't know, it's probably silly, but I feel like my hair is thinning."

She glances up at me and says, "Oh, yeah, it definitely is. I can see it from here." Come on! She's seriously sitting like a football field away.

That was a pivotal moment for me, because my worst fear was confirmed. Everyone had been telling me that I was crazy. And now I don't know which is worse—no one believing me or no one needing convincing. Anyway, Dr. Eagle Eyes told me I wouldn't go bald.

## To-Do List

Get a book published. √
Buy a nice computer. √
Rent an office. √
Launch a website. √
Pay my rent with no anxiety. √
Get a development deal with a major
   television network. √
And film studio. √
Get rich.
Quit temp job. √
Start my own company. √
Be respected for my work by certain
   conventional judges of such things. √
~~Write charming series of books about young~~
   ~~boy wizard.~~ (Fuck.)
Find boyfriend. √
Make sure he turns into fiancé. √
Marry him.
Write another book.
Get pregnant.
Have baby.
# Get a Brazilian bikini wax.
Be in good health. √
Be less depressed. √
Be less anxious.
Figure out how to avoid death.
Become a global phenomenon.

## Excerpt from **Anita Liberty's Blog**

I went to another dermatologist about my hair. Or lack thereof. This guy didn't see any evidence of thinning, but he did ask if I was losing any pubic hair. I'm like, "Wow, that's an interesting question. But I guess I wouldn't fucking know, since I just paid $45 to a large, humorless Romanian woman to rip it all out." This dermatologist also told me I wouldn't go bald. All of a sudden, a lot of people were telling me that I was not going to go bald, as if that was the most reassuring thing they could say. But I'm thinking, "There's something *before* bald that's not attractive."

I went on the Internet—the devil's tool for hypochondriacs—and one of the websites I checked said to consider styling or coloring your hair to disguise the loss. So I decided to get some blond highlights, which I think worked pretty well. But, of course, highlights are incredibly expensive and my hair is still falling out, so I feel like when I lose a hair and it's a blond one, it's like, "Huh, there goes ten dollars."

I've now become fixated with other people's hair. Anyone with thick hair I immediately resent and then I see someone with really thin hair, where I can see her scalp, and I think, "I'm not as bad as her. Yet." And I want to approach that person to talk about what we're going to do about our hair loss, but maybe she doesn't know that her hair is thinning and I'm going to come running up to her and say, "Oh yeah, it definitely is. I could see it from way over there."

## Split End

Walking down the street with my fiancé,
I see an older woman.
She has really, really thin hair.

**Fiancé:** Just keep walking.
**Me:** But . . .
**Fiancé:** It's not gonna happen.
**Me:** You don't know that.
That could be me in twenty years.
That woman might have been worried about *her* hair
thinning twenty years ago and everyone told her
she was crazy.
And now look at her.
There's a beginning to every process.
Maybe I'm just at the
beginning of that process.
**You don't know how it's all
going to turn out.**
There are no
guarantees.
**It's all a fucking
crapshoot.**
No one can
see into the
future!

## Excerpt from **Anita Liberty's Blog**

I was wrong. There is someone who can see into the future. Yesterday I took my dog to the dog psychic. The psychic held my dog and the minute she had her in her arms, she announced that my dog feels like she's not getting the recognition she deserves. And then she handed her back to me.

It was confusing to me, because my dog gets a lot of attention. From me, from Fiancé, from friends, from strangers. But I realized that when she was a puppy, we couldn't walk down the street without people stopping me to make a fuss over her. That doesn't happen so much anymore. Now she has to kind of go trolling for it. It gets a little pathetic. Like, "I'm still here. I'm still cute. Don't stop loving me because I'm getting older."

# {transference}

The process
whereby
emotions
are passed on
or displaced
from one person
to another person
(or dog).

That seals it.
I can't have children.

But apparently my sister can. My sister is having a baby! My younger sister. I don't care. Really I don't. I mean, it's not like she got married first and she's five years younger than I am and her ovaries are ripe for the picking and her life is going along exactly as she planned it with little or no angst and she got our grandmother's thick, beautiful, *never-gonna-fall-out-and-leave-her-almost-bald* hair. Also, it's not like I just got engaged and am finally enjoying the warmth of our parents' approval and admiration and the only thing that could divert their attention from the excitement of my impending nuptials would be the anticipation of their first

# GRANDCHILD.

Wait a minute. Actually, it's exactly like that.

# Having His Baby

Don't act so satisfied,
like you did something **so damned special.**

Walking around like there's a huge
neon sign on your swollen belly
flashing the words
"I am a complete woman.
I have finally fulfilled my purpose.
*Look how great I am."*

Like you've joined some special club
and taken an oath that you can't
share the big secret of life with the uninitiated.

Animals have been doing it forever.
Procreation is a fundamental element of evolution.
**It's instinct.**
Don't act like you thought of it first.

Like a Queen Bee who
believes that the drones exist only to serve her needs,
you fool yourself into thinking
that we all bow to your effect.

But don't forget,
from the drones' point of view,
the Queen
is nothing more than
a **huge** egg-carrying machine.

## Excerpt from **Anita Liberty's Blog**

I do think about having children. Mostly because everyone says that getting pregnant would help my hair grow. But also because once you're of a certain age and you're about to get married, then the thought inevitably creeps into your thinning-hair head.

**Having a baby is a big one.** Think about how much closer to death I'd feel if I had a baby. Because then I'd have brought into the world the person who's going to be saddest when I die. **Who needs that?** And I'm also not convinced that I'd be such a good parent. I don't know what you're supposed to teach your child. Is it not to have such high aspirations because then they might be let down or is the point to teach them that they can do anything so they start out with a foundation of confidence that can then slowly crumble to nothing as they encounter a series of self-esteem-crippling disappointments?

I'll say it again: **I can't have children.**

It's official; **I'm a bride-to-be.** Truly the most disturbing thing is how readily I've taken to the title, embraced practically every cliché, if not every tradition. I mean, for so long I didn't think that I would ever even get engaged, but now that I have, I feel like I've just stepped onto a conveyor belt transporting a very long procession of women numbly going through an assembly line where each of us is transformed from a normal, smart, motivated, interesting, talented, career-oriented, driven woman to a **BRIDE.**

My mother really wanted to go to Vera Wang. She just really, really wanted to go. And I thought, "What the hell? What's it going to cost me? Nothing." Nothing except for the fact that now I will be one of those women who went to Vera Wang to look for a wedding dress. And that actually amounts to a lot, considering that I always thought of myself as the kind of woman who avoids clichés. I was wrong about myself. I went. **I was Wanged.** I got a Wanging. And you know what? It wasn't so bad. I mean, she makes some nice dresses. She really does.

Of course, they could only show me four that fit my description: informal, not poufy, no sleeves, subtle. Four dresses. My mother cried at two of them. When I asked her what moved her to tears, she told me it was simply the "right neckline." I'm telling you, Vera Wang is a very good designer. So, having agreed to go to Vera Wang, the boundaries got moved. My mother then admitted to always having wanted to have the Kleinfeld experience. I, on the other hand, have lived my life determined to *avoid* the

Kleinfeld experience. On Thursday, I'm having the Kleinfeld experience. **I'm exhausted.** Really. It's just that I thought I would be able to do this in a cool and nontraditional way. But now I'm on the path and the path is well worn. And a little irritating.

# Bustier

Who else has worn this bustier?
This threadbare gray shadow of its former self?
Whose about-to-be-married breasts have also rested
uncomfortably in these scratchy cups?
Who else had to have her mother do up the kazillion hooks in
the back while she stood there in her ratty thong wearing shoes
four sizes too big?
Who else has felt her skin prickle at the humiliation?

The stories this bustier must have to tell!
This bustier has seen joy and tears.
This bustier has been stretched to its limit
and pinned to within an inch of its life.
This bustier has cradled the torsos of the rich and the not-so-
rich, the skinny and not, the ones getting married for love and
the ones getting married for money.
It has been under the right dress and, probably more often,
the wrong dress.
It has protected duchess satin, Chinese silk, organza, and tulle
from flesh.
It has caressed the bodies of a bevy of blushing brides-to-be.

I hope I don't get a rash.

It's time. It can't be avoided any longer. As much as Fiancé and I are dreading it, it's *inevitable.* All of a sudden, this whole "getting married" thing seems like a terrible idea. There's something we must endure if we want to have a wedding, get presents, declare our love, and make our union legal.

Our parents must meet. We must be present. We can't just give them a day, a time, the name of a restaurant, and then not show up. Uh . . . can we? No. We must take the first step toward joining the families. Father must take Father's hand. Mother must kiss Mother's cheek. The deal must be approved, notarized, and ordained. Fiancé and I would literally rather eat spoonfuls of live ants than sit through an evening of polite conversation with the four people who are responsible for our existences. What if they hate each other? What if there are awkward pauses? What if someone offends someone? Or, worst-case scenario, **what if they get along?** What if they actually enjoy each other's company? Plech. My parents LOVE my brother-in-law's parents. They go on vacations together. They talk on the phone. They e-mail each other. It's all incredibly cozy. **I don't do cozy.** I don't want our parents to be in *cahoots* with one another. *Cahoots* make me cringe. I'll be happy if Fiancé and I remain the only point of contact for our two families. And if all communication between the two families is channeled through the filter of me. It's the only way I can be sure to control the flow of information.

## In-Laws-in-Waiting

You know what I think is just so cool?
The idea of having another set of parents.
Especially ones that bring up a whole 'nother,
completely different, yet equally challenging,
set of issues for you.
# Neat.

One exhibits such care and patience
when choosing a partner.
I did, anyway.
This time.
And then the extra perks you don't even
anticipate, like having two more people
in your life who examine the details of
your existence through a distorted lens
fashioned from the ground remains of the
lessons they've learned from experiences
that couldn't really be less applicable to
you and the way you have chosen to spend your days.
# Swell.

I'm really looking forward to further interaction
with these two people whose passion for each
other resulted in the object of my passion.
And, besides,
I was starting to have time to waste in therapy.
Filling forty-five minutes was becoming difficult.
Now I won't have to worry.
# Nifty.

I'm thrilled.

I love my fiancé.

And it's not just one relationship.

Counting his mother and his father,

it's three-three-three relationships in one.

Buy one, get two free.

Three-for-one.

Yeah. It's a bargain.

More than I bargained for, anyway.

# Fan-fucking-tastic!

## Excerpt from **Anita Liberty's Blog**

Went to the P.O. to get stamps for the invitations (because my mother refused to let me just send out a global e-mail inviting people to my wedding) and was confounded by the choices. You have to get a 60-cent stamp to mail the invitation and then a 37-cent stamp to put on the reply-card envelope. The only choices for the 60-cent stamp were a really unattractive cherub and a heart made up of flowers that was cut out at the top in the shape of the heart. That was it. Oh, except for one of Justin Morrill. Just who the hell is Justin Morrill? (Turns out he was a prosperous merchant who helped organize the Republican Party in Vermont in 1855.) I went with the heart made of flowers and I gritted my teeth each time I placed one on an envelope. I started putting them sideways and upside down and for some reason, graphically, it looked better those ways, but isn't it a code for something when a stamp is upside down? Like "I love you" or "I put out" or "I sell drugs" or something?

Anyway, for the reply-card envelope the choices were only a little better: the American flag, the Statue of Liberty (tempting, but this isn't just about me anymore), a pink rose, and fruits and berries. I really like the fruits and berries stamps, so I decided to go with those. Somehow fruits and berries are more romantic to me than a garishly pink rose. But I do use these stamps all the time for everything, so it was a little unnerving that the reply-card envelope to my wedding invitation would sport the same stamp as the envelope carrying my check to Manhattan Mini-Storage. But I like the berries.

So my mother was addressing the invitations (she has better handwriting and I haven't written anything by hand since 1983) and I was putting the berry stamps on the reply envelopes. And I found myself making choices. It wasn't planned. I just started doing it and it went something like this: There are four types of berry stamps included on one sheet of stamps: strawberry, raspberry, blueberry, and blackberry. Turns out the blackberry is my favorite, with the blueberry running a close second. I can tolerate the raspberry, but the strawberry can just go to hell. I hate it. So I found myself deciding which berry to use depending on whose reply-card envelope I was stamping. And I thought, "This is how I should have made up the guest list. I should have only invited blackberries and maybe a few blueberries, raspberries if I had to, and absolutely no strawberries." However, the flaw in that system is that extended family got strawberries and sometimes a blackberry would go to someone who might notice, instead of someone who I felt deserved it. If there's anyone reading this who was invited to my wedding and got a raspberry or lower, I'm sorry, but now you know. (*Emily,* in your case I picked the strawberries because I thought that was your favorite fruit. Really.)

## Excerpt from **Anita Liberty's Blog**

Joe Cool. That's the name of our deejay. His real name is Joseph Anthony DiBenedetto and when Fiancé called his home number to talk to him, his mother answered. Because he lives with her. He's in his forties. Nothing cool about that, Joe. This guy isn't going to know from Wilco and Elvis Costello and OutKast and De La Soul and Britney. (Well, he might know from Britney, but he'll play her sincerely and not ironically and I'll know the difference.)

Fiancé assures me that it'll be all right. Fiancé's in charge of the music. It's his problem. But if I hear Cher singing "I Believe" at any point, it may be the quickest marriage on record. Fiancé figures that he can control the music selection by giving Joe Cool CDs and a list of songs and artists we want to hear. More importantly, he'll also give him a list of songs and artists we *don't* want to hear. Joe Cool's been told to stay off the microphone and not to use any colored flashing lights. His table has "Joe Cool" spelled out in neon, but we're going to cover that with a white tablecloth. It might take two.

I'm sure it'll be fine. Fiancé's really good at taking care of details and making sure that things run smoothly. He's really responsible and never, ever gets lazy about the finer points just 'cause he'd rather sit on the couch and read a book on the ***history of lint*** than do the legwork necessary to make an informed decision about hiring someone for the most important day of our lives.

# Advice from **Anita Liberty**

If someone changes his last name to "Cool,"
there's a very good chance he's anything but.

## Excerpt from **Anita Liberty's Blog**

We're getting married in the country. I always wanted an outdoor wedding. I never wanted a tent, but you gotta have a tent if you're going to be outdoors. Fiancé had work to do in the city, so I had to go out to the country alone to meet with some people. We've chosen a site. It's very beautiful. There are cabins on the property where we and our friends (i.e., no family) will stay. There's a gorgeous landscaped lawn in the back where we'll set up chairs for the ceremony and a tent for the dinner. It's pretty much exactly what I envisioned.

I will say the guy who runs the place is a little weird. He seems, um, overly interested in me and my wedding. His name is Garrett and he's recently divorced. He tells me a lot about himself. He told me that he gave up smoking, drinking, and eating sugar and he feels great. Whatever. He knew that I was out there alone. He asked where I was staying. I told him I was staying at a hotel in town. And that was that. Or so I thought.

I get back to my hotel and there's a message from Garrett. I call him thinking that he's calling about something to do with my wedding. Silly me. He wants to know what I'm doing for dinner. Is he actually asking me out to dinner? What kind of person owns a place that he rents out for weddings and then asks one of the brides-to-be out to dinner? And it's not like this guy is Orlando Bloom or anything. He's Garrett. I thanked him and told him that I was meeting friends. He got kind of huffy. I would laugh if it were at all funny, but it's just gross.

## Excerpt from **Anita Liberty's Blog**

Met the caterer in person today. I'd only ever talked to her assistants. The caterer is busy. Very busy. But I was anxious to talk to her face-to-face and to start giving her our ideas for the menu.

Basically, she dismissed **my ideas** for the menu for **my wedding.** Didn't like 'em. When I asked her why she didn't approve of **my choices,** she said that she knows better than I do what food will work and what food simply won't. She caters a wedding a weekend year-round, sometimes two a weekend in June and September. She's a Martha Stewart wannabe. She was a whole bunch of attitude on toast. She was a bitch. **I'm the bride.** I'm supposed to be Queen for the Fucking Day. And she's treating me like she's doing me a fucking favor catering **my wedding.**

# Hole in Fish

Wait a minute.
No, seriously.
Just hold on.
Back up.

Are you actually sitting there
telling me
that I can't have
swordfish kebabs
as part of my wedding buffet
because you can't cook fish with a hole in it?
You're telling me that the fish doesn't cook well
with a hole in it?

What?
I know you're the caterer.
I know you're the big, fancy, highly recommended,
**EXTREMELY EXPENSIVE** caterer
and you've done just about a million weddings
(including several of Billy Joel's),
but . . .
## YOU CAN'T COOK FISH WITH A HOLE IN IT?

I've cooked fish with a hole in it.
I've made swordfish kebabs.
The fish cooked fine.
In fact, they were fucking delicious.
So if you want to cater my wedding,
and I think you do,

from the way you gleefully accepted my deposit,
get the fish,
cube it up,
and

# SHOVE IT ON A STICK.

## Excerpt from **Anita Liberty's Blog**

This planning-a-wedding thing is turning out to be a huge pain in the ass. And not cheap. My parents are helping, but I'm also tapping my own resources. And seeing as Hollywood and I are taking a *break* at the moment, I'm not feeling as flush as I was.

Also, it's definitely putting a strain on my relationship with Fiancé. I'm channeling all of my creative energy into this *project* and I don't have much energy for anything else. In an effort to *reconnect,* we set aside some time for a lovely dinner, a bottle of wine, some reality television, and a little sexual role-play.

# Fiancé's Fantasy

I am a high-priced call girl.
And for five thousand dollars,
his wish is my command.

I undress slowly while he watches.
I wear black lace lingerie.
I talk dirty.
I do whatever he asks me to.
Wantonly. Willingly. Well.

# My Fantasy

The five thousand dollars.

## Excerpt from **Anita Liberty's Diary** (age 15)

*Christmas was pretty uneventful. My parents got me a really nice camera. Yay. Actually, I'm pretty upset, because I went out with John on Friday the 21st (almost a week ago) and he hasn't called me since. He said he would, too. I gave him the picture I took of him and his friend at the basketball game. He said it was nice, then he hugged me and said, "But this isn't my real Christmas present, is it? Huh, huh?" and he kept squeezing me tighter. I said, "Well, uh, no, I guess not." So I went out and bought him a scarf. It was 11 dollars. I wonder what he's getting me.*

## Excerpt from **Anita Liberty's Blog** (age 35)

Okay, so I read this and think, "It was all right there, you idiot. What were you thinking?" I can't believe I'm the same person who wrote that. Was I ever that naïve? And if I was, if I was missing something that obvious back then, what am I missing now? And today I feel so aware, so on top of it. And I know I felt that then, even though I was only 15. But here I am, twenty years later, looking back at my former self and thinking, "What a fucking idiot!"

I've been having a lot of dreams lately. Wedding dreams: wilted bouquet, marrying a stranger, ill-fitting wedding dress—that kind of thing. But I also had this amazing dream, one of those dreams that you can't believe you're having even while you're having it. I was on the beach and this older woman was walking toward me and she looked so cool. Jeans, man's shirt, short gray hair. Very older-woman chic. Very Banana Republic ad. She looked relaxed and happy. She sat down beside me and said, "Don't worry, everything's going to turn out fine."

And I was like, "Who the hell are you? How do you know?"

She smiled, turned to me, and said, "Because I'm you. Later."

Instead of feeling reassured by this cool future version of myself, I said, "What do you mean fine? Am I famous? Rich? Am I still married? To my first husband? Do I have children? When did I stop dyeing my hair? Oh, and, hey, I have hair. Am I happy? Healthy?"

She just shook her head and gave me a sort of patronizing "you'll learn" kind of look. Then she got up and walked away shaking her head. I dreamt that my older self found me pathetic. Which makes sense considering that if 35-year-old me had a chance to meet 15-year-old me, I'd slap 15-year-old me in the face.

## Excerpt from **Anita Liberty's Blog**

I'm not recognizing myself and apparently no one else is either. I'm sorry, what I mean is, I get recognized. But as someone else. There's an actress who, I guess, lives in L.A. named Rose Bishop. People don't just say I look like Rose Bishop, they see me from across a room and come running over to me, calling, "Rose, Rose." It's not until they're right in front of me that they realize I'm not her. But even then sometimes, it takes me telling them I'm not her before they realize. It's weird. People do always tell me I look great. They always seem sort of surprised at how good I look. She's a bit older than I am apparently. So I really wanted to see a picture of this Rose Bishop. Badly. I wanted to see my doppelgänger. I even thought of trying to contact her to see if she ever got recognized as me. Then a guy Fiancé knows asked me if anyone ever told me I looked like her and that was kind of the straw that broke the performance poet's back. I ranted. I raved. He backed down and said that there was really only a passing resemblance. And then he called a couple months later to inform me that this Rose Bishop was in a movie on Lifetime that week. I couldn't wait. Fiancé and I hunkered down in front of the television set to watch. It was a movie about four sisters. Rose Bishop played the mentally retarded one. Convincingly. She was hideous. Horrible. Not pretty. I vowed never to leave the house without makeup again. It was really demoralizing.

Then, one evening, Fiancé and I were watching reruns of one of our favorite shows, *Buffy the Vampire Slayer,* and we noticed Rose Bishop's name in the opening credits. As the show started, we waited to see what role my twin would be playing this time. Then we see her. She's one of a group of underlings surrounding an evil god who had come to Sunnydale to find the key to unlocking the barriers between the dimensions, so she can return to her own dimension. These underlings were gnarled, pockmarked, hook-nosed, oily creatures with beady little eyes. And they were practically bald. Not bald. *Almost* bald. With wispy, sparse tufts of hair sprouting from their scabby scalps. That was what the woman whom everyone mistakes me for was playing. That was the role that my twin auditioned for and nailed. The role she convinced producers she was born to play: a scruffy gnomelike creature with just a shot of wispy hair.

# My Most Beautiful Day

There is a day in my future
when I am going to have to be
the most beautiful I've ever been.

The problem is that that day
may already have passed.
My most beautiful day is gone.

I was in Fire Island with a boyfriend I loved.
My hair was really blond.
From the sun. From the highlights.
It was messy from the beach.
I had some color on my face,
even though I used SPF 15 way before anyone else did.
I was wearing a plain, black, sleeveless T-shirt dress.
I'm sure I had just had sex.
I wore flip-flops.
I didn't wear underwear.
I might have been stoned.
I was 23.

Now I'm 35.
And I'm getting married.
And however I look on my wedding day,
even if I look as good as I can possibly look
at this moment in time,
I will still not be the most beautiful I've ever been.
That day is long gone.
That day belongs to a young, carefree, bed-headed,
pot-smoking, tan, blond girl.

And now I'm a scruffy gnomelike creature
with just a shot of wispy hair.
I should be guarding the hellmouth,
not walking down the aisle in a white dress.

## Excerpt from **Anita Liberty's Blog**

Ya know, you're trying to plan a wedding. You got a lot of things on your mind. Menus, seating charts, writing vows, your gnomelike appearance. And people just go ahead and present you with their own agendas. It's so rude. I was supposed to give the caterer (the new caterer) the head count yesterday and yet I still have people calling and asking if they can bring guests. Hello? It's a wedding, people! It's not just some casual get-together. It's not a kegger. There's formality here. It's a wedding. You can't call me six weeks before the date and be adding names to my guest list. You already sent in your little reply cards. I've set my tables. I've counted heads. I'm trying to organize. I have lists. I have databases. I have a wedding folder, for chrissakes. I have no time for surprises. Get with the program. Of course, it was **Emily.** She wants to bring a guest because she's now dating seriously the guy she was just dating casually when the invites went out. I suppose this is a good thing in the long run, but in the short run, it really wreaks havoc on my seating chart.

And it's not just **Emily.** My sister also called me to say that she had a last-minute addition and that she and her husband were going to be bringing an uninvited guest.

## It's a Girl!

It's a girl!
It's a girl!
# Agirlagirlagirl!!!
More importantly, it's not a boy!

So now I have this tiny little Eve,
born into my life through the body of my younger sister,
who generously carried her for me for nine months
(the only time I asked her for something and she actually
**delivered).**
My sister labored to produce her physically,
and now I will labor at the development of
her creativity.
I shall act as the creative midwife,
delivering this winsome sprite
into the world of her own artistic expression.
In other words,
*I'll take over from here.*

She is beautiful.
She is perfection.
She is a tiny tabula rasa
on which to imprint
my hard-won wisdom.
It is to her that I will pass
**the torch.**
I couldn't have made her better
if I had made her myself.
The training started the moment she saw the light.

And I will reap the reward
of my careful and deliberate
influence when her first word
is neither *Mama* nor *Papa*.

but **LIBERTY.**

Everyone is annoying me. Everyone. My family, my friends, my manager, and, oh, the King of Infuriation . . . Fiancé. They can all just go to hell. I don't want to have a wedding anymore. I don't want to get married anymore. Fiancé and I are fighting like howler monkeys on crack and I just can't imagine that I'm going to look over at him on our wedding day and think, "I'm so lucky to be marrying you." More likely I'm going to look at him and think, "You're an ass-clown. Why am I marrying an ass-clown?"

I can't believe I'm actually going through with this. I hate Garrett for being so creepy. I hate the woman who's doing my makeup. I hate Lizzy for overplucking my eyebrows last night. I hate Samantha because she keeps telling me everything is going to be fine. I hate the fucking assholes at the store where I bought my dress for fucking up the alterations so many times that my dress still isn't ready. I hate my manager because my career is totally stalled. I hate everyone who thinks that celadon is the same as mint green. I hate my parents for trying to impose their agenda on my special day. I hate Fiancé because he asked me to marry him and it now seems like some horrible, awful mistake. I do not want to marry this man. What was I thinking? I don't feel very connected to this experience. Or to Fiancé. Or to myself, my needs, my feelings. It all feels pretty damned awful at the moment. And I don't even have time to write. It's just three weeks before my wedding day and I have to keep going and going and planning and calling and faxing and e-mailing and paying and I'm exhausted and cranky and angry and sad and frustrated and not really very happy.

We started writing our vows last night.

# Anita's Vow

I don't know what you're expecting from me,
but I can't promise to be nice and supportive for ever and ever
in every possible scenario and situation.
I just can't. You know I don't like to make promises I can't keep.
However, I can vow to try.
And I will try. Hard.
I vow that I will *try* to be nice and supportive
for ever and ever in every possible scenario and situation.
Although, if I'm being completely honest,
some days I might try harder than others.

Mitchell. After such a long time of not thinking about him, I've started thinking about him. But why? Why now, mere weeks from the day of my wedding?

I Google him. Which is what one does in today's world. And I find nothing of note. It looks like he lived in Los Angeles for a while, but that he doesn't live there anymore. But that's really all the Internet has for me. And it's not enough to satisfy my curiosity. The Internet is unable to tell me the things I really want to know. Is he happy? Is he healthy? Does he ever think about me? Is he still with Heather? Are they married? Do they ever talk about me? What do they say? Is she pregnant? Do they already have a child? Or two? Does he know what I do for a living? Did he read my first book? Does he still have his hair? Where is he right this minute? What is he doing? Who is he with? Where will he be on the day of my wedding? Does he know I'm getting married? How does that make him feel? Does it make him feel anything? Is he capable of feeling anything? How instrumental was he in getting me to this day? How much did he help to shape who I am? Does he ever think that he made a horrible mistake dumping me? Is he ever sorry for the way he did it? Does he ever wish that he had apologized? Just once? Just fucking once?

You know what? I still hate the guy. No matter how much time passes, as fulfilled and happy as I get, I'm still going to be able to work up a decent rage at my ex-boyfriend. And I don't want to hear anything about it. I don't want anyone shaking his or her head and feeling sorry for me that I just can't let it go. I have let it go. I don't sit around stewing about Mitchell all the time, but when he pops into my head, which he does occasionally, because he is a part of my past, I pause for a moment and think about him. And when I do, I remember how much I hate him. I hate him like I hate lima beans. I don't spend time thinking about how much I hate lima beans, but if they're right in front of me, I get a little grossed out.

If I am determined to continue to be who I am once I am married, I have to accept that hating Mitchell is as much a part of me as the blood that runs through my veins or the hair on my head (or in my shower drain).

# {closure}

The distance measured
vertically between the top
of a rock formation
and the lowest contour.

## Excerpt from **Anita Liberty's Blog**

My bridal shower's this weekend. What will that be like? My mother and sister are planning it. They're having a "tea." I hate tea. They don't know me. They don't care what I want. It's all about them. It feels like this wedding's all about anyone but me. It's like I'm planning a big party for everyone else and I'm going to go into it really stressed and everyone else will go into it calm and happy and enjoying all the details that have woken me up at fucking four in the fucking morning every night for the past three weeks. It's not worth it. And what if I am making a horrible, terrible mistake? Can I walk away? Right now? That would be very dramatic. I'd have a lot of explaining to do. But wouldn't that be better than locking myself into a life with a howler monkey who doesn't know his howler monkey ass from his howler monkey elbow? I really don't know. What I do know is that I'm going to a party this weekend being thrown for some bride-to-be who has nothing in common with me. I have no choice but to prepare myself for disappointment.

## Advice from **Anita Liberty**

Yeah. Okay. This is a tough one.
You don't know everything all the time.
Sometimes people surprise you.
Like if you're thinking that your bridal shower
is going to suck because you think that no one
knows you and you're not going to get the kind of
bridal shower that you deserve and you walk into
your mother's home and there on the table, along with
the salmon sandwiches and glass pitchers of iced tea,
is a centerpiece your mother made for the occasion.
It is a doll. She is a bride. With a white dress.
And a bouquet of tiny white flowers.
Her cheeks are soft pink.
Her hair is rust-colored yarn. She has pearl earrings.
But on her head is no tiara or veil or sparkly barrette.
On her head is a small green crown.
The Statue of Liberty's crown.
A bride maintaining her freedom,
her sense of independence, her liberty.
See? You don't know everything all the time.

# Excerpt from **Anita Liberty's Blog**

My manager called. The network wants me to rewrite the pilot. This time alone. The movie studio wants me to do a draft of the screenplay. Without Mr. A-List attached. Everything's moving forward. But I'll be doing it all alone. Which is good. Because that's how I've always done my best work. How ironic that I'm ten days away from becoming legally and (I hope) irreversibly coupled.

## Excerpt from **Anita Liberty's Blog**

Have arrived in the country a week before the wedding to get everything ready. Things seem to be going fine. We went to check on the site and saw Garrett on a riding mower. He was smoking, drinking a beer, and had a pack of Nutter Butter cookies in his lap. He glared at us. Why? 'Cause I wouldn't go on a date with him the month before my wedding. Yeah. He should be annoyed.

Fiancé and I went to get our marriage license. At the county clerk's office, we were handed our license and a sealed plastic bag filled with items useful for a new wife. Dish-washing soap. Laundry detergent. Spot remover. Facial scrub. Chap Stick. Perfume. A sewing kit. A preconceptional care brochure. Hand cream. Mouthwash. Air freshener. Oh. Okay. All that soul-searching and introspection and torment I went through in order to feel the slightest bit qualified to make the decision to marry, there was no need. It was a huge waste of time and energy. But how could I have known that all I ever required was waiting right here for me at the county clerk's office? In a small sealed plastic bag. **Now** I feel ready to enter married life.

# To-Do List

Get a book published. √
Buy a nice computer. √
Rent an office. √
Launch a website. √
Pay my rent with no anxiety. √
Get a development deal with a major
  television network. √
And film studio. √
Get rich.
Quit temp job. √
Start my own company. √
Be respected for my work by certain
  conventional judges of such things. √
~~Write charming series of books about young
  boy wizard.~~ (Fuck.)
Find boyfriend. √
Make sure he turns into fiancé. √

## Marry him.

Write another book.
Get pregnant.
Have baby.
Get a Brazilian bikini wax. √
Be in good health. √
Be less depressed. √
Be less anxious.
Figure out how to avoid death.
Become a global phenomenon.

# Perfect

My wedding day was a perfect day.
Our wedding day was a perfect day.
     Once we'd fired the first caterer and found the second.
It was transcendent and pure.
     Ignoring the fact that the guy who owned the site
     came on to me.
Everyone looked beautiful. Charmed.
     So what that the hotel's booking policy bordered
     on harassment?
Supreme goodness. Absolute delight.
     We're sure that the tent company won't actually take us
     to small claims court.
The day was more than we'd allowed ourselves to imagine.
     The favors arrived completely fucked up, but the
     company replaced them with, oh, minutes to spare.
All was wholly exquisite. Untouched. Marvelous.
     Because on the morning of that day, there was a moment
     when my fiancé saw me in the distance.
     He kissed the palm of his hand
     and then held that hand to his heart
     as he smiled at the woman who was about to be
     his wife.
That day changed my standards dramatically.
Because now I know what it's like to experience a perfect day.
Not alone. Together.

# To-Do List

Get a book published. √
Buy a nice computer. √
Rent an office. √
Launch a website. √
Pay my rent with no anxiety. √
Get a development deal with a major
   television network. √
And film studio. √
~~Get rich.~~ (Never gonna happen.)
Quit temp job. √
Start my own company. √
Be respected for my work by certain
   conventional judges of such things. √
~~Write charming series of books about young
   boy wizard.~~ (Fuck.)
Find boyfriend. √
Make sure he turns into fiancé. √
Marry him. √
Write another book. √
Get pregnant.
Have baby.
Write inevitable book about
   motherhood. (Preorder yours on
   www.anitaliberty.com or www.amazon.com
   today!!)
Get a Brazilian bikini wax. √
Be in good health. √
Be less depressed. √
~~Be less anxious.~~ (Never gonna happen.)
Figure out how to avoid death.
Become a global phenomenon.

# To-Don't List

Forget who I am.
Lose my edge.
Fuck it up.

So.

The honeymoon's over. Actually, the honeymoon ended while we were still on the honeymoon. We fought. Several times. Not just bickering. Really angry fights. What's wrong with us? What's wrong with our marriage? **No one** fights on their honeymoon. **No one.** It never happens. It's a sign. A very, very bad sign. I kept telling Husband (apparently, *First* Husband) how bad it was and how no one, *no one,* fights on their honeymoon and that we must have an extremely fucked-up relationship for us to fight on our honeymoon. **Our honeymoon!** The point in one's marriage that's supposed to be the happiest point. If you can't get through that without fighting, what hope does your marriage have?

Samantha just called. She wanted to hear about the honeymoon. I said Paris was beautiful. What she really wanted to know was how much we fought. She then told me that everyone fights on their honeymoon. It's a rite of passage. Oh. Uh-huh. Ya think she might have told me that *before* the fact.

**One Last Piece of Advice from Anita Liberty**

If you fight on your honeymoon, no big deal.
It doesn't mean that your marriage is doomed
or that you've just made some horrible mistake.
There's a lot of anxiety around planning a wedding.
Getting married brings up a lot of emotions.
Once you're on vacation, some of those emotions
might spill out on each other in the middle
of the Luxembourg Gardens
or the Rodin Museum
or in front of Jim Morrison's grave.
Really. Don't worry about it.

# It's perfectly natural.

# {end}

I know what you've come to expect from me.
I know that I set up those expectations.
So I'm sorry if I'm disappointing you,
but this time the end is a happy one.
A terribly, terribly happy one.

(Oh, calm down. I'll be back. Just imagine what
I'll be like when I have someone camped out
in my uterus for nine months. It won't be pretty.)

{end}

Right. The acknowledgments. The book is finished. I'm done writing. You're done reading. And now it's time to see who supported me in this ambitious endeavor. The thing about acknowledgments is that sometimes when I pick up a book I skip right to the acknowledgments page to get a sense of the author. Is she thanking her significant other? Her dog? Her baby? (Like the dog or the baby did anything to help the author write her book.) Does she know anyone I know? Does she know anyone famous? Is she good enough to have gotten any grants? Or be invited to any writers' colonies? Do the acknowledgments indicate any favors that might have been done to aid in the publication of her book? You can see that I read a lot into acknowledgments, and why it's hard for me to go thanking the people in my life willy-nilly without giving it some serious thought. Also, I'm writing this after my manuscript has been edited and copyedited, and now this is going to have to be edited and copyedited and that's going to be very frustrating for my editor and my copy editor because they were probably just expecting a list of names. But that's not my style. And they should know that by now.

Having said all that, here's whom I acknowledge:

Mark Tavani. He's my editor. I have to thank him. But he deserves thanks. He's smart, sensitive, and intuitive. And he makes me feel good about myself.

Arielle Eckstut. She's my book agent. I have to thank her, too. But Arielle did more than just find this book a home— she was this book's doula. And, because of her hard work, the manuscript came in healthy and alert.

Cindy Ambers. My manager. My ally. My confidante. She is an unwavering source of strength and wisdom and friendship. But if you're looking for a manager, don't go looking her up at Verve Entertainment in Los Angeles, because she already has a lot of other pesky clients who take up her precious time.

Sanyu Dillon, Ingrid Powell, Paul Taunton, Brian McLendon, the Copy Editor Who Wishes to Remain Anonymous, and everyone else at Villard for everything they've done and everything I know they're going to continue to do for this book.

My mom. She's my mom, for chrissakes. Of course I'm going to thank her. Even though when I saw my manuscript on her nightstand one morning, I asked her if she'd read it. She said, "Oh yeah. I'm almost done!" Since I'd given it to her just the night before, I was surprised and touched. She said, "It's a wonderful book. A *wonderful* book." Her response was so serious and sincere. I felt so validated and happy. And then I realized that she was talking about *The Kite Runner*, which was next to my manuscript on her nightstand. But she swears she loves my book, too.

My dad. My dad taught me more about writing than anyone else. He told me, when I was a teenager and we were working on my personal statement for my college applications, that I should write things down exactly as I hear them in my head. It was fantastic advice. And I've made a career out of it.

Now I just have to list a bunch of people who offered me support and resources and insight whenever I asked. (Please note that this is a list of people who contributed in a specific way to the successful completion of this book. It's not just a list of people I like. Although I do like all these people.)

Amy Brenneman, Deborah Brody, Michael Calleia, Elizabeth Cashour, Elizabeth Connors, Ellen Dubin, Elizabeth Giamatti, Elizabeth Hannan, Jennifer Hart, Neeltje Henneman, Janice Maloney, Kristin Marting, Mary-Louise Parker, Linda Reitzes, Spencer Robinson, Nancy

Rose, Steven Saden, Brad Silberling, Jason & Randy Sklar, and JTW.

And, finally, I'd like to acknowledge CDoov and the Monkey, for being such spectacular friends that (uncharacteristically) I can't find the words to describe my gratitude. (Tears are coming to my eyes. How sappy is that?)

ANITA LIBERTY is the author of *How to Heal the Hurt by Hating*. She has been performing her work before live audiences for the past decade. She has developed and written a bunch of television pilots and a couple of screenplays. Her website is www.anitaliberty.com. Anita Liberty lives in New York City with her husband and—*spoiler alert!*—her daughter. Oh yeah, and—*another spoiler alert!*—her real name is Suzanne Weber.

notes:

notes:

notes:

notes:

notes:

notes:

notes:

notes:

notes:

notes:

notes: